STUDENT-FRIENDLY GUIDES

Excellent Dissertations!

Second Edition

Excellent Dissertations!

Second Edition

Peter Levin

Open University Press

Open University Press
McGraw-Hill Education
McGraw-Hill House
Shoppenhangers Road
Maidenhead
Berkshire
England
SL6 2QL

email: enquiries@openup.co.uk
world wide web: www.openup.co.uk

and Two Penn Plaza, New York, NY 10121-2289, USA

First edition published 2005, this edition 2011

A catalogue record of this book is available from the British Library

ISBN-13: 978-0-33-523861-3
ISBN-10: 0-33-523861-0
eISBN: 978-0-33-523863-7

Library of Congress Cataloging-in-Publication Data
CIP data applied for

Typeset by RefineCatch Limited, Bungay, Suffolk
Printed in the UK by Bell and Bain Ltd, Glasgow

Fictitious names of companies, products, people, characters and/or data that may
be used herein (in case studies or in examples) are not intended to represent any
real individual, company, product or event.

The *McGraw·Hill* Companies

Contents

Part 3 The 'middle period'

Part 4 The 'end game'

Tables

Producing a dissertation — Read this first!

Are you required, as part of your studies and along with taking taught courses, to submit a dissertation or long essay of 10–30 thousand words or so? Are you expected to create it by yourself, in your own time, and to hand it in by a set deadline? Will it be given a mark that counts towards your degree result? If so, this book is for you. But you may also find it helpful if you're starting work on something longer, like an MPhil or PhD thesis. Much of the advice I offer – for example, on selecting a subject or topic, creating a literature review, and managing your work – applies whatever level you're working at.

Many students, facing for the first time the task of producing a dissertation, feel at a loss. They don't know where to start; they feel unprepared. Very largely, I believe, they are in this situation not through any shortcomings of their own but because their experience of education up to that point has indeed not prepared them for the kind of independent work that producing a dissertation calls for. Perhaps this applies to you, too. What has been going on?

To answer this question I think we have to look at the 'model' of education to which students are exposed. It seems to me that there are basically two models of education to be found in higher education institutions in the UK, and indeed in UK secondary schools as well. In the first model, students are treated as 'receptacles', as containers to be filled up with knowledge (largely factual knowledge, supplemented with a certain amount of know-how). Courses are 'delivered' to you, and your task is to take in and retain as much of the material in them as you can – and then to reproduce it.

The second model is quite different. In this model, students are treated as 'detectives': you are presented with puzzles and problems to solve, and are expected to acquire not only puzzle-solving and problem-solving techniques but also ways of hunting for and piecing together clues. In other words, you have to acquire not only the necessary techniques but also the initiative, alertness, perceptiveness, intuition and 'sixth sense' that good detectives possess. If you are given coursework assignments to do in your own time, these will test whether you have acquired these 'detective qualities'. However, you will be extremely fortunate if you have teachers who take the trouble to make these explicit and teach them to you. If your teachers don't do this, then your coursework assignments will be testing you on qualities that you haven't actually been taught. (This happens in secondary education, too.) If you find yourself getting poor marks for such assignments and don't understand why, that could be a major contributory factor. And it doesn't bode well when you are faced with the need to produce a dissertation.

Here's a thought. Producing a worthwhile dissertation requires you to be a detective. Consequently, if the education you have experienced up to now has given you no training in detective work, it should be no surprise if you feel at a loss when you're required to submit a dissertation. Your experiences of having knowledge 'poured' into you will be of absolutely no use to you. So do appreciate that you are now in the business of acquiring a new, different method of learning. One of my aims in writing this book is to help you to do this.

The book starts from the recognition that producing a dissertation is a twin-track enterprise. It involves both:

- undertaking a project – doing the work (including detective work), and

- presenting your findings – writing up your work.

This book is designed to assist you with both these activities. In particular, it is designed to help you *manage* your project work and your writing up, and to be *aware* of what is going on for you.

You may find that you get very little help from your teachers with the management aspect of producing your dissertation. This may be because the task is regarded as an examination, in which you have to work unaided. But, even if producing your dissertation is regarded as a learning experience, in which you are entitled to assistance, your supervisor may not be good at giving it.

Academics are not renowned for their management skills, nor for nurturing students who are grappling with tasks that are new to them. You may be fortunate and have a supervisor who is supportive and able to empathize with you when you're struggling. At the other extreme, your supervisor may be completely unable or unwilling to engage with you at an emotional level. If your supervisor is of the latter type, I hope this book may fill the gap to some extent. At the very least, it should provide some reassurance that the problems you face are not unique to you, and some moral support at those inevitable times when your spirits and energy flag.

Every dissertation has to comply with certain requirements. These vary from subject to subject, department to department, and institution to institution. And no dissertation comes into being through exactly the same process. Consequently no worthwhile book of this kind can give 'one size fits all' advice. My approach, therefore, is to highlight the questions that you need to ask to discover for yourself what it is that you have to do, what choices are open to you, and how to choose one course of action rather than another. In a sense, I am offering a compass and other navigational aids to help you find your own way, rather than a map which I am telling you to follow. However, you will find many practical suggestions and recommendations in the following pages.

In the academic world, as in the 'real world' outside, every task is what you make it. You can put a lot of thought and effort into it, or you can put in very little. You could treat 'doing a dissertation' as no more than composing an over-long essay, but something more than that is required for a decent dissertation. Making a precis of six books might just possibly get you a pass mark, but it certainly won't win you any prizes. You will need to do something more intellectually demanding: exploring, investigating, testing, analysing, explaining, evaluating, making a critique, and so on. I aim to help you work successfully at this level.

Finally, here are four reasons why it is worth putting some time and effort into creating your dissertation.

- The 'dissertation challenge' offers you an opportunity to get your teeth into a subject that interests you and to pursue it in some depth. It's a chance to step off what may feel like the week-by-week 'treadmill' of term time in academia.

- If you feel that conventional examinations are not a good test of your ability, you can take advantage of your dissertation to show what you are capable of.

- A good dissertation will assist your supervisor to write a good reference for you: a sentence or two highlighting the qualities that you've demonstrated will be far more helpful in getting you an interview than some stock phrases about doing well in your studies.

- If you can talk intelligently in an interview about how you tackled your dissertation challenge, and what you learned from it, you will be well on the way to being offered the job you're after.

I wish you success!

Peter Levin

Introduction

My overall purpose in writing this book is to help you go about the task of producing a dissertation that will get you an 'excellent' rating in a final-year undergraduate examination or a taught master's examination in the UK. I have been prompted to write this book chiefly by the questions that students working on a dissertation have asked me. For example:

- What are the examiners looking for?

- How do I choose a topic and a title?

- How should I manage my time?

- My supervisor has told me I have to start by writing a literature review? Is this really the thing I should do first?

- How much help can I get from my supervisor?

- How original does my dissertation have to be?

- How do I structure a dissertation?

- How many chapters should a dissertation have, and how long should they be?

- Which is the best referencing system to use?

You'll find answers to all these questions, and many others, in the pages that follow.

This book is the second edition of *Excellent Dissertations!* Since the first edition was published, in 2005, I have continued to learn at first hand about the problems that students face, and I have rewritten a number of passages for this second edition and added some new ones to take account of what I have learned. In some cases students have shown me that I needed to express more clearly what I want to communicate, and in others I have had further thoughts. This new edition also benefits from the fact that, since 2005, many universities and departments have published dissertation handbooks for their students; it has been instructive to read these and note the many differences – as well as similarities – between them.

Reading dissertation handbooks, what has struck me most forcibly is that while they are mostly pretty good on the mechanics – complying with the rules and regulations – and most contain snippets at least of sound advice about how to manage the job of producing a dissertation, they are much less good at helping you to *think* about what to do and how to do it. That leaves a gap, which I hope this book will go some way to fill. Incidentally, a number of handbooks stress the importance of thinking *critically*. No institution should object if you turn your critical eye on your dissertation handbook itself.

There have been other changes, too, in the past five years. Much more information is available on the World Wide Web, and advanced forms of software – to help with finding information and referencing, as well as supposedly tracking down plagiarism – have become available. The present generation of librarians are the people you should consult for help here. For the author of a book such as this one, there is also the problem that URLs that need to be cited are often huge and unwieldy, and consequently inappropriate for the medium of a printed book. I have attempted to deal with this problem by providing instead a term that you can put into a search engine and have the site offered to you at or close to the top of the list of results. I have placed these search terms between arrowheads, like this: $>$ $<$.

Part 1
Preliminaries

Formal requirements and arrangements

Before you start work on producing your dissertation, you *must* do your 'homework' to discover what is officially required of you and what arrangements have been made for supervision, etc. In a sense, this is your first research task, and it needs to be done thoroughly and systematically. Equip yourself with the answers to the questions below.

Is there a 'dissertation handbook' that I can consult?

Nowadays it is common practice to issue students with a dissertation handbook that contains information about your dissertation: arrangements for supervision, requirements for presentation and submission, etc. If you haven't been given a dissertation handbook, you should at least have a course handbook containing a section on the dissertation.

It will help to be clear about the status of the information in your handbook. It is likely to comprise both official university and department regulations, and guidance notes from your faculty or department. Regulations *must* be complied with – and you are likely to be penalized if you don't comply with them – but guidance notes may merely have the status of advice, with no automatic penalty if you don't follow it.

Why do I have to do a dissertation?

Does your handbook make clear the institution's purpose in requiring you to submit a dissertation? You are likely to be told that it gives you an opportunity to do some independent work, and that most students find it a valuable and worthwhile experience. But that leaves two main possibilities. One is that the purpose of the dissertation is merely to give you a 'take home' form of examination, one where you pose your own question, set your own time limit, and can write with your books, off-prints and your computer screen in front of you, but get no help from your teachers. The other is that the purpose is to give you a learning experience, where you have the opportunity to carry out a piece of independent research and delve into a subject more deeply than you have time for on your taught courses, *and* you get help from your teachers in doing that. If the purpose isn't clear, look at what your handbook says about arrangements for supervision.

If your supervisor's role is simply to get you started – to discuss your proposal, recommend reading matter, etc. – after which you're on your own, then the purpose of the dissertation is essentially to test you. And if you get marked on your proposal – and in some places you'll be marked on an oral presentation of your proposal and/or on your literature review, too – then testing is very much the purpose of the exercise. Such ancillary testing may be presented as a way of giving you an incentive, but (a) most students don't need such threats to make them work, and (b) it is very difficult for your supervisor to be simultaneously an assessor and your guide, philosopher and friend. One role requires a degree of aloofness from students; the other requires a degree of mental closeness. If your supervisor is compelled to be your assessor, his or her ability to help you learn will inevitably be impaired.

If, on the other hand, you are offered regular meetings with your supervisor, and if he or she will read drafts – of even just a chapter or two – then doing the dissertation is evidently envisaged as a learning experience for you: there should be a good chance that you will actually get some tuition in how to undertake a project, how to do research. If your handbook includes some kind of statement of 'learning objectives', this too suggests the latter purpose, and you should feel entitled to seek the help that is implied.

What is the 'word limit' for my dissertation?

You will certainly be told at some point – in your dissertation handbook, if you have been given one – that your dissertation must contain no more than a certain number of words. This is the 'word limit'. In all probability there will be a penalty, such as a number of marks deducted or a refusal to read and mark beyond the word limit if your dissertation exceeds it, so it is imperative that it should not do so.

This instruction is less straightforward than it appears, however. You need to know whether the word limit includes the following:

- the title page – this may carry, as well as the title and a 'submitted in fulfilment' statement, a declaration that the work is your own and perhaps another to the effect that you have complied with an ethics code; there could easily be 80 or 100 words on your title page

- the list of contents (chapter headings)

- acknowledgments

- abstract (or executive summary)

- footnotes or endnotes

- appendices

- bibliography

- words in tables and diagrams.

Few dissertation handbooks cover all of these in their information about word limits. If you notice any omissions that could affect you, ask about them.

You may perhaps be informed that there is, in addition to a maximum word limit, a minimum limit: your dissertation must have at least a certain number of words. The purpose of this seems to be to emphasize the importance of undertaking a project of some substance, rather than to warn you of a likely danger: while many dissertation handbooks spell out the penalties attached to exceeding the maximum word limit I have yet to find one that tells you what the penalties are for not attaining the minimum.

Does my dissertation have to be in a particular physical 'format'?

You will almost certainly be told what information you must provide on your title page, and how pages must be laid out: font size, margins, line spacing, etc. You will almost certainly be told how the hard copy of your dissertation is to be bound, and whether you are required to submit an e-copy as well. You may also be told which referencing system to use.

How long do I have until handing-in, and what is the procedure?

You should be told the latest date (and time) by which the dissertation has to be handed in (submitted), and where. You should automatically be given a receipt for it. You should also be told what the penalties are for handing in late. Examiners are obliged to treat all candidates the same, and this should rule out accepting a late hand-in without penalty unless there are medical or compassionate grounds. You will almost certainly be told that problems with your computer or printer will not be accepted as an excuse for late submission. So you *must* back up your work – every draft! – and not leave printing until the last minute.

What do I have to do about choosing a subject and title for my dissertation?

Check with your dissertation handbook to see whether it sets out any limitations as to your subject. Does it have to be one on which there is a substantial body of relevant literature? (And does this literature have to be in English?) Does the subject have to be one that is related to a taught course that you've been following, and/or one that a teacher in your department is willing to supervise? If so, you need to know.

There may be a set procedure, with a deadline, for submitting a proposal for your dissertation project and having it approved, and there will certainly be a set procedure, also with a deadline, for submitting your dissertation title and having that approved. Ask about these procedures if the information is not provided for you. You may have to submit your proposal before you have been officially allocated a supervisor, in which case it will be sensible for you to approach members of staff informally for advice on it, especially if you are trying to choose between two or more different possibilities.

What are the arrangements for allocating a supervisor to me?

Arrangements for allocating supervisors to students vary widely. You need to be aware of what the formal arrangements are in your department, and in particular what opportunity you have to make an informed choice of supervisor for yourself. In some places you will be encouraged to 'shop around', to talk to academics in your department – some of whom may have a list of dissertation projects that they offer students – and in effect find a supervisor for yourself. In others, you may be required to hand in a dissertation proposal and then wait to see who has been allocated to you.

Even in the latter case, there is a great deal to be said for being proactive, taking the initiative yourself. Bear in mind that there may be a quota system in operation to share out students among supervisors and limit the number that any one supervisor has. So you may find yourself in competition with other students for a supervisor who specializes in your chosen field and/or for a supervisor with a good reputation. Accordingly, from the earliest stage, think about possible subjects, make some notes on possible alternatives and identify possible supervisors. (To do this, find out their areas of interest and recent publications, and, if you can, talk to the previous year's students about their experiences of supervision.) Then go and talk to them. If someone is interested in your subject, and helpful, and you feel there's a good chance that you could establish a constructive relationship with them, then you could ask them if they would be willing to supervise you. They will probably remind you about the formal procedure, but behind the scenes they may be able to have a quiet word with the person in charge of the allocation system.

In some circumstances, provision may be made for joint supervision by two supervisors. This might be normal practice for students whose dissertation project takes the form of a work placement, with one supervisor being in the department and the other in the workplace, or when one supervisor can be a methodology expert and the other a specialist in your particular field. It may be worth exploring this possibility if you think it could be advantageous for you.

What arrangements are there for supervision?

Once you have a designated supervisor, you need to know what help you are entitled to expect from him or her, and at what stages. If the dissertation is effectively a take-home examination, you may be entitled to expect your supervisor to give assistance in selecting a subject and finding reading matter, but not to comment on drafts of your dissertation. If the dissertation is supposed to provide a learning experience, your supervisor may be able to provide guidance with methodology and to comment on early drafts of chapters or sections. For more on getting help from your supervisor, see Chapter 3.

How will my dissertation be marked?

Some handbooks provide you with the 'marking scheme' that examiners will be using when marking your dissertation. This aims to show you what qualities your dissertation needs to have to get a certain grade. If you do an internet search for > "dissertation handbook" "marking scheme" < you may find that on one course a master's dissertation is said to need to have the following properties in order to be awarded a mark of 65–69:

Grounded in thorough research and demonstrating a high level of skill in the critical use and interpretation of a substantial body of primary sources. Clear evidence of originality. Intelligently structured argument. Correct use of a scholarly apparatus.

Observe the 'judgmental terms' here: *thorough* research, *high* level of skill, *substantial* body of primary resources, *clear* evidence, *intelligently* structured argument. These all involve a subjective judgment on the part of the examiners. These terms could apply in many subjects: try to work out what they would mean for you. To some extent you can do this by asking your teachers questions. You may learn something from comparing past dissertations (if you are allowed access to them), especially by comparing those that scored high marks with those that didn't, although your institution will probably not allow you to see dissertations that were placed in the middle range or below.

There's actually a quite subtle lesson here. In effect, high marks are awarded to students who have shown in their dissertations that they have learned to distinguish thorough research from patchy, to recognize a skilful piece of work, to appreciate the need to base their research on a wide rather than narrow range of primary sources, to tell clear evidence from fuzzy, and to know when an argument is 'intelligent' (which presumably means logically reasoned, complete and watertight). Those students haven't merely mastered technicalities – they have acquired a 'feel' for their subject. They have learned to think like their teachers, to see the world through their eyes. This is something that isn't consciously taught on higher education courses. It isn't learned by taking copious notes in lectures. It's hard to say quite how it is learned without using analogies such as 'osmosis', but you will, I think, have a head start if you are alert and open-minded, and try to 'read between the lines'. So you don't merely pay attention to what is written: you ask why it was written, who it was written for, why it was written in that particular way, and so on.

Unlike the marking scheme cited above, there are some that make extensive use of very general judgmental words such as 'satisfactory', 'good' and 'excellent'. These are of no use to you whatsoever. You are being offered – tautologically and lazily, in my view – the advice that to get a 'good' mark you have to submit 'good' work. You need to discover from your teachers – who will be your examiners – how they recognize good work when they see it.

For more on examiners' expectations, see Chapter 2, 'Pleasing the examiners'.

Who will mark my dissertation?

Almost certainly your supervisor will be one of your examiners, since he or she is likely to be the person in your department who knows most about your subject (topic). Good practice dictates that there will be a second examiner from your department, although this is not universally the case. Good practice also dictates that whichever examiner marks second does so 'blind', i.e. not knowing what mark the first examiner has given, although that is not always the case either.

When the two 'internal' examiners have marked your dissertation, they will (usually) meet to agree a mark. If they cannot agree, or if the agreed mark is a fail or a distinction (master's) or first class (undergraduate), or if it falls on the borderline between classes, the dissertation will be seen by a third examiner, the 'external', who will come from a different institution, and he or she will read the dissertation and the reports of the internal examiners and make a recommendation. This will go to a meeting of the Board of Examiners, which will take the final decision. No mark is ever definite until the Board has concluded its meeting.

Will my dissertation have my name on it when it is marked?

It is good practice nowadays in UK higher education that examinations are marked 'anonymously' – that is, candidates are identified by number and not by name . The purpose is to guide against prejudice, conscious or unconscious, that an examiner might have if you are known to him or her, or if your name suggests that you are a member of a particular social, ethnic or religious group. But not every institution follows this good practice where dissertations are concerned.

Your dissertation handbook will tell you whether to put your name or your candidate number on the front cover of your dissertation. Of course, even if you are identified only by number your supervisor, who will be the first or second marker, will know who you are by virtue of recognizing your work. But this may not be the case for the other internal examiner, and certainly won't be the case for the external examiner. If you are required to put your name on your dissertation and you have reason to suspect that there could possibly be prejudice in your case, you could raise the issue, preferably in a way that does not single you out as a troublemaker – for example, by asking your class representative to put it on the agenda for a meeting of the staff–student committee.

Can I see dissertations written by past students?

In some places and some departments you are allowed to see dissertations written by past students; in others you aren't. If you are able to see them, look at several, and make sure you know what grades they have been given: you don't want to take your cue from a poor example. You should treat other people's dissertations as offering you a starting point, no more. Following a past dissertation's treatment slavishly, however good a mark it has been given, is definitely not a recipe for your success. Every dissertation needs its own, particular, tailor-made treatment.

Consistency

You might like to check that you and your fellow students have all been given the same information and advice, especially if the 'official' information – whether it's contained in a dissertation handbook or provided in some other form – is very sketchy. It may be that different supervisors put different interpretations on written codes, or exercise their discretion differently about how much help to give, or informally give different advice about procedure. There's no harm in satisfying yourself that the playing field is level.

2

Pleasing the examiners

What examiners like to see

While some examiners do have fixed ideas about how dissertations in their subject should be written, so their standpoint is basically critical, in my experience the majority have an attitude that *appreciates* the qualities to be found in good dissertations. Command of the subject matter is of course essential, but examiners also like to see – and will reward – a dissertation that reveals some or all of the following qualities on the part of the author, the project and/or the dissertation itself:

■ The ability to conceive of a purposeful, feasible and manageable project, and to frame a concise, meaningful question or questions.

■ The ability to choose and apply a clear and appropriate methodology for the project.

■ An awareness of the subtleties of the subject, an eye for relevance and significance, and the ability to see connections and to handle a complex subject without oversimplifying it; these tend to go with an appreciation of the broad context within which the project is situated – an ability to see simultaneously both the 'big picture' and significant details.

■ Evidence that the relevant literature has been read, digested and appropriately made use of, with the project having been conceived within a scholarly context and conclusions likewise related to that context.

■ Some evidence of the ability to think independently and critically; 'originality' may or may not be a requirement for undergraduates and taught postgraduates, although if it is demonstrated it will be appreciated (a project that incorporates fieldwork or uses very recently published data will be original almost by definition).

- Thoroughness – evidence that work has been done carefully; that proper attention has been given to detail; that the subject has been treated comprehensively (e.g. no omissions in its coverage, no significant aspects left unexplored); and that the study has been properly completed (no loose ends remaining).

- A systematic, logical and appropriate structure for the dissertation, together with clarity, neatness and consistency in layout, presentation of data, referencing, etc.

- Persuasive advocacy in subjects where you are expected to put forward a point of view and argue for it.

- Evidence that the dissertation is indeed the work of the person submitting it.

- Compliance with the formal requirements; failure to comply with the word limit or hand in by the deadline will usually result in a penalty – loss of marks, or worse.

What examiners don't like to see

It follows that examiners are unhappy if they observe that the above attributes are not present when they should be. Additionally, in general, examiners *don't* like to see the following:

- Use of your own personal experience ('anecdotal evidence'), unless you treat it in a rigorous manner.

- Use of the words 'I think' or 'I believe'. Statements of your thoughts and beliefs do not constitute valid elements of reasoning in an academic dissertation. If your thoughts are based on evidence, as they should be, offer this evidence and demonstrate what follows from it. Likewise, if your beliefs are based on certain values, make these explicit.

- Straying outside your discipline. While taking a technique that has been developed in one academic field and applying it in another may demonstrate that you are a gifted lateral thinker, this may not be appreciated by the examiners. If you are an economist, you will almost certainly be expected to deploy the techniques and reasoning of an economist, not those of a sociologist or psychologist, for example. Likewise, if you are an archaeology graduate who is doing a master's in anthropology, it may well be prudent to keep your archaeological knowledge and training well in the background. But do check with your supervisor whether this is the case. There are a few enlightened academics who recognize the benefits of taking of a cross-disciplinary approach to a subject, but unfortunately many do not.

- Poor use of English, especially if the result is that the meaning of what you write is not clear. Your writing in English does not have to be sophisticated or elegant, but you must use words accurately – i.e. you must use the correct word for the meaning you want to convey – and your grammar, punctuation and spelling must be acceptable to the examiners. 'Chatty', colloquial language and slang will not be appreciated: they don't lend themselves to precise expression.

- A lack of structure, which might be shown in an absence of a logical 'flow' from chapter to chapter, rambling paragraphs, repetition, new material introduced in the conclusions, and general untidiness. Some academics find untidiness and inconsistency merely annoying, but many find it infuriating: very few will fail to notice them, and probably the great majority will feel that untidy presentation and inconsistency are indicators of work done in a rush and not thought through properly, and will mark down the dissertation accordingly.

3

You and your supervisor

You depend on your supervisor

Your supervisor is your point of contact with the upper echelons of the 'power structure' in your institution. You depend on him or her initially for advice about your subject and how to tackle it, and for approval of your dissertation title; then for feedback on your work, if that is permitted (i.e. if the dissertation is treated as a learning experience rather than a mere test); and finally in their role as a marker of your dissertation.

Rights and expectations

Your dissertation handbook or other document provided to you should contain some kind of statement that sets out your rights with regard to supervision. For example, you may have the right to meet with your supervisor once a month, or to have one or two draft chapters read and commented on. The word 'rights' won't necessarily be used in this context. Expectations may also be implied, again falling short of using the word 'rights' – look out for statements like 'Supervisors also undertake a pastoral role …', which do this.

You and your supervisor are both human beings, and there are limits as to how far 'one-to-one' human interactions can be 'legislated for'. It follows that if there is to be a relationship between the two of you that is helpful to you, even if your supervisor is available to you only while you're choosing your subject and title, you may have to take an active part in creating it.

Observe your supervisor

A good rule is to observe your supervisor carefully, from the moment you first meet him or her. Is this someone who sees their role as that of 'guide, philosopher and friend'? Someone who takes the trouble to put you at your ease, who listens attentively to your concerns, and doesn't end a meeting before you have agreed when you will next meet and what work you will do before your next meeting. Such people do exist, and they can make being supervised a very rewarding experience.

But keep asking yourself questions. Is this someone who has their own agenda with regard to your choice of subject? Someone who is clearly anxious to get meetings over with quickly? Someone who doesn't probe areas where you express uncertainty? Who gets embarrassed if you talk about personal matters? Or who behaves in a warmer and friendlier manner than you feel is appropriate? If so, you will do well to be wary.

Formulate your tactics

If your experiences with your supervisor are consistently negative, to the extent where you feel you have no confidence in him or her, you may be able to request a transfer: your institution should have a formal procedure for this. But you should do what you can to avoid matters getting to such a point. Here are a few suggestions.

- Don't take things personally. If your supervisor is a self-centred obsessive, preoccupied with his or her own research as some academics are (indeed, as they have to be if they are to fulfil the targets set for them in today's academic world), their behaviour won't be the result of any antagonism towards you specially.

- Identify your supervisor's strengths and take advantage of them. If he or she isn't much good at providing encouragement and sympathy but is an expert in their field, use them as a consultant. See if you can find someone else – a friendly academic, a fellow student or a group of fellow students – who can provide you with the emotional support that everyone who's working on a project and dissertation needs at some point.

- If your supervisor does have 'consultant qualities', the way to get his or her attention is to intrigue them. So, before a meeting, do as much preparatory work – reading, investigating, thinking – as you can, and try to come up with a dilemma or puzzle that will challenge them. Seek their advice on it. Whatever you do, don't act helpless. Don't ever ask to be told what to do. Your supervisor isn't your parent or even your instructor.

- It may be that the person appointed as your supervisor is not a specialist in your chosen subject. Perhaps you have chosen a subject in which there are no specialists in your department, or there is one but he or she is unavailable. Don't kick yourself for not having chosen a different subject. While non-specialists won't be acquainted with all the relevant literature, they will often be able to help with methodology and planning, and their experience in the wider field may make them good people to try your ideas out on. They're also less likely to be offended if you go and talk to experts elsewhere.

- Try never to leave a meeting with your supervisor without fixing a date for your next meeting and without agreeing what you should do next. This should help to ensure that when you do next meet you will have something to report, and that it won't take your supervisor by surprise.

- During meetings with your supervisor, take notes. As soon as possible after each meeting, write them up, so you have a record of the advice given and any agreements reached and decisions taken. It does sometimes happen that supervisors forget what they told you at a previous meeting and give advice that contradicts advice they gave earlier. Having a record will help you to resolve such contradictions. And if, unhappily, your relationship with your supervisor does break down, your records will strengthen your hand and your case when you seek to remedy the situation.

Part 2
Getting started

4

The 'twin track': your project and your dissertation

The distinction between project and dissertation

In creating a dissertation, you have two things to do. You must:

- Undertake a project – for example, a project to find the answer to a research question, to test a theory or hypothesis, to evaluate an action or proposal, to formulate a critique.

- Write up your project in the form of a dissertation, in which you present your findings, discuss their significance and offer your conclusions.

It is easy to lose sight of the distinction between project and dissertation, between undertaking your project and writing it up. If you think of your task as being to *write* a dissertation, or to *author* a thesis, you are already blurring that distinction: you're losing sight of the fact that you have a project to do. And if your project is one of reading and thinking – as in history, law or philosophy – rather than fieldwork or laboratory work, you can easily lose sight of the distinction, because writing will be part of your project work as well as your writing up. And then you are exposed to the danger that the 'linearity' inherent in any piece of writing makes you think linearly when doing your project, so you plough on forward rather than thinking laterally and reiteratively.

Oddly, the distinction between project and dissertation seems to be lost on some academics and institutions. You can see this from the emphasis that they put on dissertation titles. You may be told to suggest a title to your supervisor and to discuss it with him or her, and to formally submit your proposed title to your institution, but not invited to discuss the subject and methodology of your project in any detail. This despite the fact that you can't possibly be clear about the suitability of a title unless you have first clarified your thoughts about the project you intend to undertake and checked out its feasibility.

Project and dissertation usually develop together. Most students find not only that their project work feeds into their dissertation, as you would expect, but also that the process of writing up generates thoughts and ideas that feed into their project. So don't feel that you have to complete your project before you do any writing. Indeed, many dissertation handbooks stress the importance of starting to write early. It will pay you to keep asking yourself, while you are doing your project: 'What shall I be able to write about this? What will it contribute to my dissertation?'

While your project and dissertation will 'grow up' together, in some respects the project must come first, of course. You have to do some work before you have anything to write up. You have to be clear what your subject and methodology are before you can arrive at your title. And you must be reasonably clear about your plan of work before you can rough out a plan for your dissertation.

At the same time, though, you must bear in mind the dissertation requirements while planning your project. The deadline and the word limit for the dissertation will limit the scope of your project. And your dissertation will need to incorporate a discussion and conclusions, so it is important to design your project to maximize the likelihood that you will come up with results that you can report and interpret in your discussion and conclusions.

It may help you if you draw a distinction in your mind between two kinds of writing: 'writing as thinking' and 'writing as presenting'. 'Writing as thinking' is essentially part of your project work. 'Writing as presenting' is all about writing up your work into a dissertation.

Writing as thinking

By 'writing as thinking' I mean the writing that you do as part of gaining understanding of your subject. This includes jotting down thoughts, ideas and questions that occur to you when you read something that might be relevant to your work; or when you see how you could make use of a technique you've read about; or when you have to make a choice between alternatives and make a list of the pros and cons of each one; or when you're simply trying to make sense of something that's puzzling you. Simply keeping a log can help you in gaining understanding, as well as help you to keep track of your progress. And writing as thinking will play an important part in clarifying what's in your mind. As William Faulkner is reputed to have said: 'I never know what I think about something until I read what I've written on it.'[1]

You're actually doing something very subtle and sophisticated here. You're starting with a complex, jumbled 'cloud' of material in your head, and out of it you're trying to draw something that is essentially structured, with its components connected by chains of reasoning. This process is far from being a merely mechanical one. Think about the language we use to describe it: 'The idea popped into my head', 'I suddenly thought there must be a connection', 'I had a flash of inspiration', 'It just struck me', 'Got a problem? Sleep on it', 'I did some brainstorming', 'It was the result of lateral thinking'. That process is not one that you will find consciously taught, unless you are extremely fortunate, but you will find yourself acquiring it if you can manage to learn to think like your teachers.

So when thoughts and questions occur to you, or you come across potentially useful quotations or experimental results, make notes. (Keep pen and paper by your bedside to record thoughts that come to mind when you wake in the early hours.) Play with ideas. Look at a wide range of literature: it is a good way of exposing your mind to stimuli. And make a habit of reading and rereading what you have written. (This is what academics do, incidentally.) Your notes will be for your eyes only, so it doesn't matter if they look untidy: the important thing is that you know where everything is, and that you keep your mind open and receptive and fertile. In due course, you'll be using the latest versions of your notes as the basis for your write-up, for your dissertation, as you move into 'writing as presenting'.

Writing as presenting

Writing as presenting is all about transforming the notes you have made into 'dissertation format', and doing so with your readers – i.e. the examiners – very much at the forefront of your mind. So you'll be assembling your notes into a linear sequence, and checking to and fro to make sure the sequence is logical. You'll be adding new material to fill gaps and taking out any repetition that you find. There will be passages where you yourself are clear what you mean, but when you distance yourself and ask whether someone coming fresh to it would understand it, you realize that more clarity is needed, and you have to spell out your train of thought carefully. In effect, you are now making your piece of writing 'reader friendly'.

Doing this may well feed back into your writing-as-thinking process. In clarifying matters for your reader you may find that you are clarifying matters for yourself, too, and generating new ideas as you do so.

Later on you'll be working in 'editor mode'. You're making sure that your style is consistent throughout, and that paragraphs aren't too long or too short. You're cutting to meet the word limit. You're checking that your references are all present and correct, and in the same format.

First steps

The first steps towards producing your dissertation require you to do a number of things. You have to explore the literature, make a shortlist of possible subjects for your project, select your preferred subject, think about the methodology you will use and the materials that you will apply your methodology to, and devote some thought to time management and planning. The following chapters deal with these in turn.

5

Project and dissertation: exploring the literature

By 'the literature' I mean academic publications: books, articles, and theses or dissertations by academics or other scholars. I'm not including in this category official and other formal publications, or data sources and reference handbooks, or articles in professional journals and magazines, or writings that constitute the subject matter of your project: these all come under the heading of 'materials', and I deal with them in Chapter 10.

How to read

Reading causes huge problems to many students. Several factors contribute to this. One is that when they come to university they take it for granted that they already know what 'reading' is and how to do it: you open a book at page 1, start reading, and keep going – word by word, sentence by sentence, paragraph by paragraph and chapter by chapter – until you've reached the end, when you can stop. A second factor that makes reading problematic is the sheer quantity of literature that exists today on most subjects; and a third factor is that much of this literature is written in 'academic-speak', the specialist language used by academics in that field.

Given that academic learning is largely 'driven' by the written word, when you're faced with this mass of literature, what can you do? As I've suggested in *Write Great Essays!*,[2] where you will find a great deal of advice on reading academic publications, the first thing you must do is to 'reframe' your notion of what 'reading' is. Think of it not as soaking up great masses of stuff, but as conducting a kind of treasure hunt to find the specific points that you need. And the second thing you must do is to explore the literature, systematically.

Exploring the literature is different from writing a literature review. Don't confuse the two. Writing a literature review involves writing an essay that presents an overview of the relevant literature, brings out points that are important for your project, and possibly incorporates a critique of the literature too. (For more on writing a literature review, see Chapter 14.) But exploring the literature is a matter of discovering what there is and what you might use, of searching for and tracking down books and articles that might be relevant. Don't try to master the literature in depth at this stage unless you come across something that is absolutely central to your proposed work, otherwise you'll be seriously at risk of getting bogged down.

Tracking down potentially useful academic publications

Listed below are some ideas to help you track down potentially useful academic publications.

- Make the most of any relevant reading lists that you have been given for your taught courses. Starting with the most recent publications listed, check out their references and bibliographies for leads to other books and articles.

- Make full use of your institution's library. Take advantage of any training courses it runs in how to find useful publications, and consult the enquiry or help desk when you need assistance in finding your way around. If you haven't already done so, learn to use its computerized catalogue, and find out how to use its computer system to carry out searches for publications on your particular subject. Find out how to access the catalogues of other academic libraries.

- Find out what specialist libraries there are in your field – many professional institutes and institutions maintain libraries at their headquarters – and investigate the possibility of gaining access to them. A student card and/or a letter from your head of department or supervisor may be needed for them to let you in. They may have journals that your institution's library doesn't.

- Identify the most relevant journals in your field and browse through recent numbers, checking out not only articles but also book reviews and letters to the editor for mentions of your subject.

- If there are prominent writers on your subject, look them up on a search engine, including general ones such as Google. You might find a reference to a recent paper, or a recent or forthcoming lecture or conference appearance, that's worth following up.

- You might – just possibly! – find some useful leads through Wikipedia, but bear in mind that articles on the Wikipedia website are *not* academic publications. *Never* cite one in your dissertation.[3]

There are no short cuts. Don't expect anyone else to do this work for you. Once you've done some scouting around – but not before – consult your supervisor to see if there's anything you've missed. You are much more likely to get useful help if you have already shown some initiative. The same applies if you want to consult experts elsewhere. An email along the lines 'I am making a study of … What should I read?' is likely to be deleted instantly.

Exploring the literature: what to look for

Exploring the literature is not the same as ploughing through it. You need to 'skim' over the literature, as if you were skimming over the ground on a magic carpet, keeping an eye out for shiny pieces of treasure on the ground. So let your eyes skim over the pages and keep a lookout for whichever of the following might be of use to you:

- Differences of opinion among writers: might there be scope for you to identify the points on which they disagree, or differences in the assumptions they have made or the evidence they have used, or defects in the logic of their arguments?

- Theories, hypotheses, conjectures, surmises: do these amount to more than speculation, guesswork? Are they consistent with other theories etc. and with empirical observations? Can you think of ways of testing them?

- Concepts and definitions: has the writer used concepts that might help you to make sense of whatever you want to study? Do these go beyond the use of abstract language – academic-speak – to describe something?

- Generalizations: are these warranted? How were they arrived at? Can you think of a way of testing them?

- Questions: has the writer given satisfactory answers to questions that he or she has posed? Would your answers to those questions be different?

- Statements about causal connections: has an observed effect been attributed to a single cause where there might have been a number of contributory causes and/or enabling factors? Has the writer revealed the mechanisms at work? Has the writer used a particular model of 'explanation' but not spelled out what it is? Might you be able to differentiate the motivations, resources and opportunities that lie behind observed human behaviours?

- Puzzles, mysteries, inconsistencies, things that don't add up: is there something that challenges you to solve or enquire into, or that brings out the ingenuity in you?

- Techniques: has the writer carried out experiments or used methods of measurement or analysis or engagement with a subject that you could apply to different subjects or in different contexts? Do you have any criticism to make of the validity of his or her findings or conclusions?

- Value judgments: has the writer concluded that a policy, say, was good or bad, harmful or beneficial? Do you agree? What are the criteria the writer used in reaching that judgment? Would yours be different?

- Recent developments: what has changed? Does it amount to a step-change, or an incremental development, or a change in direction? What might be its significance?

- Gripping accounts: in some fields you may find inspiration from accounts of research – for example, ethnographic studies of certain societies, action research into a community campaign, or qualitative research carried out in schools.

Start compiling a bibliography and collecting publications

A dissertation's bibliography is a list of the publications consulted by the writer. Every dissertation must have one. Start compiling yours straight away. Every time you come across a potentially useful publication, add it to your list. See Table 1 on page 33 for the details of each publication that you need to make a note of. Do be sure to write down full details of each one: it can be a frustrating business trying to recapture these details later. You can always delete items from your list in the writing-up stage if you end up not having used them.

Students tackling a dissertation project invariably find themselves building up a collection of publications on their subject. And they find themselves consulting a number of them more than once. Understandably so: it is a common experience that as you learn more and think more about your subject, you keep returning to your collection of publications, and each time you do so you see things that didn't register with you when you read them before.

So don't rely on being able to find publications in the library when you want them, or on web pages always being available, and available in the form they had when you first found them. Don't merely bookmark pages: save them on your computer and back them up too. And don't try to skimp on publications: it could well turn out to be an economy that you will regret. Set aside some funds for buying books, photocopying chapters and articles, and printing out material you've downloaded from the web. You can save yourself paper and ink/toner by copying web page content into a word-processor document and deleting extraneous material before printing. You can also copy the URL into that document, and add the date you accessed the web page.

Once you've chosen your subject, start collecting. Incidentally, if you're photocopying a chapter from a book, check whether there is anything potentially useful in other chapters, such as the introduction and conclusions: you may want to photocopy those too.

You are of course free to highlight, underline, sideline and make marginal comments on any books or papers that are your own personal property, and I do encourage you to do that. (If you've been well brought up and it goes against the grain to mark a book, use a soft pencil – so you can erase it later – and semi-sticky labels: Post-its make excellent bookmarks.) You'll find it's a great help in digesting the material and ultimately making the subject 'yours'.

You should be aware that there are legal limits on how much photocopying you may do free of charge. Your institution almost certainly holds a licence with the Copyright Licensing Agency that permits photocopying within certain limits only. The rules say:

The proportion of a work that may be photocopied consists of:

- one whole chapter from a book
- one whole article from a journal issue
- a short story or poem (not exceeding 10 pages in length) from an anthology
- one whole paper from a set of conference proceedings
- one whole report of a single case from a volume of judicial proceedings

---

or 5 % of any of the above, whichever is the greater.[4]

Record details of publications

Citing sources will be easier to do if you make a habit of recording their details at the time when you take notes from them. When you're photocopying pages from a book save yourself some work by photocopying the title page, too, because it will have some of the details you need (don't forget to add the year of publication and number of edition on to your photocopied title page). In Table 1, I list the details you'll need to record about 'paper' sources, i.e. books and articles.

I include the ISBN and ISSN in Table 1 because they may help readers in tracking down a book or journal very quickly in an academic library's online catalogue. Bizarrely (in my opinion), none of the standard referencing systems requires the inclusion of that piece of information, although the ISBN system was introduced in the UK in 1967 and adopted for international use in 1970, so it has been around in the UK for more than 40 years and as long – or nearly as long – elsewhere.

For an article on a web page you will need to record:

- the name(s) of the author(s) and the title of the article

- the URL (uniform resource locator) of the page, otherwise known as its web address

- the date on which you accessed the page

Table 1   Details to record about your 'paper' sources

For a 'unitary' book (i.e. written as a whole, not an edited compilation)	For a chapter in an edited compilation book	For an article in a journal
The name(s) of the author(s)	The name(s) of the author(s) of the chapter	The name(s) of the author(s)
The title and subtitle	The title of the chapter	The title of the article
The year of publication	The title and subtitle of the book	The title of the journal and any standard abbreviation of the title
The edition, if not the first	The name(s) of the editor(s) of the book	The year of publication
The publisher	The year of publication	The number of the volume of the journal
The city or town where the publisher's main office is situated	The publisher	The part number of the journal and the month (or season) of publication
The number(s) of the relevant pages	The city or town where the publisher's main office is situated	The number(s) of the relevant pages
	The number(s) of the relevant pages.	
The book's ISBN (International Standard Book Number)	The book's ISBN (International Standard Book Number)	The journal's ISSN (International Standard Serial Number)

- if the web page is actually a reproduction of a 'paper' article, the details of the journal as in the right-hand column in Table 1.

It is sensible to copy and paste the URL into a document to guard against errors in copying by hand, especially if the URL is one of those monster database-generated ones whose rhyme and reason are known only to the webmaster.

Be sure to store the web page electronically, and also to back it up – you might want to print it out, too – so you have it to refer to if the page is subsequently altered or becomes unavailable. And watch out for line breaks (*never* insert a hyphen, as this will change the URL) and for underscores concealed by an underline. You can minimize the need for line breaks by using a narrow font, such as Arial Narrow or Helvetica Narrow, and a smaller pitch than you normally use.

When exploring the literature, all you want to know is whether a publication that you come across might be useful to you. When you find something that you think is potentially useful, write a little note to yourself, giving the details of the publication (as in Table 1) and your thoughts on how you might make use of it. File your note somewhere safe.

Don't start writing your literature review yet

At this early stage, do not spend valuable time starting to write your literature review. It's possible that your supervisor will ask you to show him or her a literature review early on, but try to get out of this. There are four reasons for avoiding this task. First, you don't know, when you're starting work, which pieces of literature will be relevant to your future work and which ones will not. Second, you are quite likely to uncover fresh sources as your work proceeds; it is not a good use of your time to redo work each time you find a new source. Third, it is only when you are well advanced that you will be able to be properly critical of the books and articles that you are using. Fourth, the proper place for critical comment on the literature is – in my (not uninformed) opinion – in the 'Discussion' chapter of your dissertation, when you can consider it in the light of the results of your project.

Writing a literature review when you aren't yet on top of your material is one of the most mind-numbing, brain-deadening, sleep-inducing activities known to students. If your supervisor is insistent, try to get away with producing just a list of sources, and a brief note on the content and possible value of each.

6

Project: making a shortlist of possible subjects

What grabs you?

What do you actually want to do for your dissertation project? If it's going to entail laboratory work, you have probably identified the phenomenon that you want to examine and probably, too, the technique(s) that you want to use to examine it. If you want to do fieldwork among people in a particular setting or locality, you probably have in mind something that you want to find out about them. Or you may have a general idea about the subject you want to tackle. Perhaps you say things like 'It would be interesting to look at the Human Rights Act 1998' or 'I'd like to write about the Crimean War.' Statements like these are not specific enough to get you going – and they say nothing about the approach you're going to adopt – but they do give you a starting point. What will *your* starting point be?

The formal requirements for your dissertation will impose some limitations on your choice of subject. For example, you may be barred from using material that you have used previously in an essay; check with your dissertation handbook for any restrictions of this kind. You will certainly be required to produce a dissertation that is your own work, and it would be sensible not to take a subject that you know someone else has taken unless your approach would be different and/or you have good grounds for thinking that you would come up with different results and conclusion.

Your subject does not need to be one that no-one anywhere has ever tackled before, and your dissertation ought not to be judged on whether it makes an original contribution to knowledge (that's for a PhD), but in practice it is almost certainly worth trying to find a combination of subject and approach that breaks some new ground. Your exploratory reading should help to get you brainstorming along those lines, and here are some more questions that could help. (At this stage, don't worry about how to choose a single subject – concentrate for now on drawing up a shortlist of possibles; anything from two to five will be a good number.)

- Is there something that you've come across in one of your taught courses that you didn't have time to explore properly but would like to know more about? Have you ever asked a teacher a question and not been satisfied with the answer? Now's your chance to see if you can put together a better one. Checking out past exam papers might give you an idea or two.

- What's currently happening in your field of study? In most fields there's usually something new or recent to be investigated. Is there a new book or article with new ideas, the implications of which you would like to explore? Is there a disagreement, with protagonists expressing different points of view? This offers scope for exploring how it is possible for different views to be held and the possibility of reconciling them. Has a new theory been published, one that you could test? Has a new technique become available, one that you could compare with or apply alongside existing techniques? If a new product has become available, could you explore its properties and evaluate its usefulness?

- Has a new source of data become available, offering a rich vein of material for analysis? Do you have contacts outside university giving you access to materials to which you could apply methodologies that you have learned?

- Has someone published a case study that it would be interesting to replicate in a different context, allowing you to compare its findings with your own, and to test – and possibly refine – their methodology?

- Is there some literature in your field that you are critical of, or a train of thought you would like to pursue? Do you feel you have something to contribute to a current debate? Or is there a gap of some kind that you think you could fill? (A gap by itself may not be very inspiring, however – see if you can formulate a question or puzzle that would help you to fill it.)

- Do you have some personal experience that you would like to draw on? This is legitimate, and will certainly help you to meet any requirement to do with originality, but there are traps that you must avoid. You must not merely give an account of your experience but place it in the context of other studies and/or theories. And you must avoid being judgmental: confine your judgments to your discussion and conclusions, and make clear if you can the values on which they are based. It's a good idea to take other people's experiences as your subject, and draw on your own to give you insights into their experiences.

■ If you're an international student in a social science field, would it be interesting – and feasible – to make a comparative study between your home country and the UK, or to investigate a UK-centred subject which would generate useful lessons that you could take home with you?

Warnings

A word of warning: avoid subjects set in the future, like 'What will happen if/when …?' The future is not susceptible to investigation, and although you may be able to get somewhere by extrapolating into the future you'll get very few, if any, marks for speculating about it.

Another word of warning: do not let your supervisor talk you into taking on a subject that you are not comfortable with. (Unless, of course, you want to find out at first hand what it's like to have a nervous breakdown.) Students do sometimes think that their supervisor knows best, and take his or her advice despite their own misgivings, especially if they are taking a master's in a field different from that of their bachelor's degree. But some supervisors have their own agendas and some are not at all good at putting themselves in a student's shoes. Get as much informed advice as you can (or can accommodate – too much advice can be very inhibiting) but at the end of the day trust your own instincts and take your own decision.

At the end of this exercise you should have a shortlist of two to five possible subjects. They can be quite general at this stage. Once you have your shortlist, you can start thinking about which to choose. That's the subject of the next chapter.

7

Project: choosing your preferred subject

Checklist for choosing

Given your shortlist of possible subjects, you have to make a choice between them. Before you can do this, though, you must do some work on each of them. Here is a checklist of six questions to ask about each possible subject. For the one you end up choosing, you need to be able to answer 'yes' to all six of them.

- Is this subject specific enough?

- Is this subject narrow enough?

- Do I have a clear aim?

- Do I have a feasible approach to this subject?

- Is there a good chance that I'll come up with an interesting conclusion?

- Am I enthusiastic about this subject?

Make your subject specific

It's very likely that if you have identified a possible subject in general terms, you are thinking of it in abstract, 'woolly' language. You need to express it in specific, 'concrete' terms. So translate all academic-speak words into down-to-earth language: describe your subject in terms that will enable anyone to recognize it when they see it.

Narrow your subject down

Narrowing a subject down involves setting boundaries to it. This might involve limiting it to one or two case studies (studies of particular cases), geographical areas, historical periods, organizations, physical phenomena, writers or socio-economic groups, for example. Bear in mind the unavoidable trade-off between breadth and depth: the broader your subject, the shallower your project must be.

For example, take the question that students often ask: 'How many case studies should I make?' Consider the options: one, two or three. Tackling just one case study will allow you to go into greatest depth. This might be particularly good for testing a theory – it takes only one demonstration that the theory does not hold to invalidate it. It might also be particularly good for generating insights into the mechanisms, say, that the proponents of this theory seek to uncover. Tackling two case studies must have the effect of reducing the depth that you can go into, because your time and the number of words permitted are limited. On the other hand, it will allow you to make comparisons between the two, if they have some features in common, and you can explore the use of the theory in explaining the differences that you discover. Tackling three case studies will reduce your depth even more, although it could yield some more interesting comparisons; you will have to make your own judgment as to whether the loss of depth is outweighed by the gain in breadth.

Identify a clear aim

Identifying a clear aim involves getting clear in your mind what it is that you want to learn about your subject. You might want to explore something you have read that puzzles you: a change in a writer's views over time, perhaps, or the effect on him or her of a particular experience. You might have come across a purported explanation that you haven't found convincing, or a theory that you think needs testing, or behaviour that requires to be explained, or a collection of observations that need to be made sense of, or something that requires you to make a judgment, e.g. of strengths and weaknesses. Your aim will serve to give you a focus for your project.

Identify a feasible approach

Identifying a feasible approach to your subject requires you to ensure that you have a methodology (see Chapter 9) that will enable you to achieve your aim, the materials to which you can apply your methodology (see Chapter 10), and the personal resources (such as time and ability) that you will need.

Envisage arriving at an interesting conclusion

It will be very helpful if you can visualize, in at least a broad outline, an interesting conclusion that you might come to, and get some indication from your supervisor that this conclusion is likely to arouse the examiners' interest.

Be enthused by your subject

Whatever the subject you choose, it's really important that you have some enthusiasm for it. Producing a dissertation is hard work, and you'll need some enthusiasm to sustain you when the going gets tough.

An example

For example, you might be saying to yourself 'I want to consider the issues that professionalization addresses.' Now apply the six questions in the above checklist.

Is this subject specific enough? No. The words 'issues', 'professionalization' and 'addresses' are abstract, academic-speak – before you can work out how you are going to undertake your project they have to be translated into specific, 'concrete' terms. That is to say, you have to be able to say how you distinguish 'issues' when you see them, or at least to give some concrete examples of issues. Similarly with 'professionalization' (which could mean either the state of 'being professional' or the process of 'becoming professional') and 'addresses'.

Is this subject narrow enough? No. As it stands it is far too broad, because it is so unspecific.

Do I have a clear aim? No. All you've said is that you're going to 'consider' issues: this could amount to nothing more than producing a stream of commentary – possibly mere 'waffle' – on the subject. It conveys nothing at all about what you want to learn.

Do I have a feasible approach to this subject? Without a specific subject and a clear aim, it's not possible to draw up a feasible approach.

Is there a good chance that I'll come up with an interesting conclusion? It's impossible to say.

Am I enthusiastic about this subject? In my experience, people who cannot give clear and positive answers to the first five questions tend to be depressed rather than enthusiastic about their project.

Let's try again …

A more specific subject. A more specific formulation of your subject could be: (a) actions taken at national and local level in the past ten years directed towards raising the professional standards of members of the social work profession; and (b) the number of cases of children placed on at-risk registers in the past ten years who have subsequently suffered a non-accidental injury.

A narrow enough subject. Being more specific, your subject is already narrower, but you will probably need to narrow it down further by confining yourself to one or two regions or localities.

A clear aim. You're asking a clear question: is there a correlation between the actions taken to raise the professional standards of members of the social work profession and the number of children placed on at-risk registers who subsequently suffered a non-accidental injury? And you would be asking a clear subsequent question: What has brought about the correlation, or lack of it, that you find?

A feasible approach. To judge whether your approach is feasible you will need to know at the very least whether (a) you can identify actions that have actually been taken to raise professional standards – this may depend on whether these have been documented and, if so, on whether you can gain access to the relevant documentation; and (b) you can gain access to the data you need on the children with whom you are concerned. Your search for an explanation of your findings would probably involve interviewing people; you would need to ensure that you conformed to an ethical code of practice and to be sure you have the time and skills needed to arrange and carry out interviews, transcribe your notes, and compile a report on them.

The chance that you will come up with an interesting conclusion. Whether you find a correlation or not, I think you could well have something interesting to report and something worth trying to explain.

Am I enthusiastic about this subject? Certainly you now have more grounds for enthusiasm.

Make your choice

If you have started off with a shortlist of possible subjects, my suggestion is that you ask the six questions in the checklist about each of them. Then compare your lists and make a choice. If this is difficult, ask your supervisor for help. Even if it seems straightforward, it will be worthwhile asking for comments. Your supervisor may well be able to point out aspects that haven't occurred to you. The fact that you have done your homework first will help to get you a sympathetic hearing.

When you have chosen your subject, write yourself a note with your answers to the checklist questions above. So it should cover: description of subject (must be specific enough); boundaries of subject (must be narrow enough); aims (must be clear enough); feasibility (must be 'doable'); reasons for thinking there's a good chance of an interesting conclusion; and why you feel enthusiastic about this project. Pin this note up somewhere where you'll see it every time you sit down to work. Update it whenever you change something. You'll find it useful in keeping yourself on track, and particularly valuable when you come to write the 'Introduction' to your dissertation. It may also serve as a 'proposal statement' if you are required to submit one.

8

Dissertation: choosing your title

Once you've begun thinking about your subject, start to draw up a short list of alternative titles, especially if you are able or required to discuss your title with your supervisor. You will get a more useful reaction if you offer a selection than if you offer only one, and if you have already done some thinking about the pros and cons of the various alternatives.

Bear in mind that your title must be informative, self-explanatory. Someone who is looking at a list of dissertations, maybe in a library catalogue, wants to be able to see at a glance whether yours might be of interest to them. So avoid choosing a title that is likely to mystify a reader rather than reveal what your dissertation is about. Resist the temptation to be clever. If in doubt, try out your title on a range of other people. Tell them you're writing a dissertation; they will almost certainly ask you 'What's it about?', and then tell them your title. If they react with bafflement, you may need to make it more straightforward.

If you like the idea of a snazzy, eye-catching title, you may wish to take advantage of the 'colon convention' that allows you to have a double title, with the two parts separated by a colon, e.g. 'Manners makyth man: a cross-cultural study of social etiquette at ballroom dances'.

It ought to be acceptable for your title to take the form of a question, with a question mark at the end, e.g. 'Why did Bismarck resign?', but check with your supervisor that it is indeed acceptable.

Ideally you should be permitted to submit no more than a 'working title' when you start work on your dissertation, and have the opportunity to finalize it when it is clear where your project is taking you. But if you have to submit your title at an early stage and won't have the opportunity to change it later, make sure you choose one that is not too restrictive, so it can accommodate changes in direction or emphasis that you may later find necessary. For example, 'Local democracy in the United Kingdom: a case study' offers more room for manoeuvre than 'Local by-elections in the London Borough of Newham 1998–2002'.

9

Project: methodology

To carry out a project successfully, you must be absolutely clear what methodology you are using, and how you are using it. (I use the word 'methodology' to denote principles and ways of working as well as specific methods and techniques.) Please note: if you are going to arrive at conclusions you cannot avoid having a methodology, because it is methodology that will get you there. You might close your eyes to this fact, but even if you see yourself as doing no more than 'writing' your dissertation, and not carrying out a project, if you are doing some reasoning – such as choosing what sources or materials to rely on – you have a method of working.

It is beyond the scope of this book to go in any detail into the methodologies employed by the whole range of academic disciplines. However, if you are to make a success of managing your project there are certain general questions about methodology to which you must have satisfactory answers. In this chapter I distinguish different kinds of subject and the methodologies that go with them, and offer a checklist of questions to ask about each of them.

Kinds of subject and the methodologies that go with them

It is possible to distinguish several kinds of subject, although any categorization will necessarily be somewhat rough and ready. Each calls for its own particular methodology. I have listed these in Table 2.

Investigating a phenomenon in which you are not involved

Although the variety of phenomena that take place or have taken place in the world is infinitely vast, there are – I suggest – some common

Table 2 Project subjects and methodologies

Subject	Methodology (what you do)
A phenomenon in which you are not involved, such as a physical process or any human activity that took or has taken place before you start work	You investigate it; you collect evidence about it, describe it, and seek to 'understand' it or 'explain' it, or generate a theory about it
A phenomenon in which you are personally involved, such as ongoing activities in a social, political or workplace setting	Engage with others and record events and subjective impressions (participant observation, action research, qualitative research); aim to generalize from your experience
A theory, including a theoretical model, conceptual framework, generalization or hypothesis	Test it for consistency with empirical observations, consistency with other theories, etc.
A proposition or a philosophical argument	Tease out its implications, test it for logical consistency
A proposal for a design, policy or action	Evaluate it: explore how it would 'work' in practice, and set out and apply criteria for evaluating it
An issue or problem; a 'how to … ?' question	Explore it and, if possible, (re)solve it
A technique	Try it out and see what you can do with it
A creative work	Analyse it and make a critique of it
A theme	Discuss it
A thesis	Argue in support of it

principles that apply to investigating them and some common questions to be asked about them.

First, before you can investigate a phenomenon you must have at least some description of it. There must be features of it that have registered with you, either because you have observed them directly or because you have read about them. And your description must be concrete enough to enable you to recognize it when you see it or read about it. An abstract, all-embracing academic-speak definition won't do. If you describe your phenomenon as 'international trade in goods and commodities', or 'the effect on one financial market of events in another', you have something that you can recognize. If you describe it as 'globalization', you don't.

When we describe a phenomenon, we do so by picking out those features that strike us as 'salient', as having significance. Ask two people to go into a room, one after the other, and then to come out and describe the room, and they will give different descriptions. To one, the large number of books and office equipment will be the salient features. To another, the salient features will be the low ceiling and smoky atmosphere. Use your reading to check that your perception of salient features does not overlook any that other writers have found significant.

Second, be clear whether you are investigating a single, 'one-off' phenomenon; or one that has some similarities with others; or a recurring, reproducible one. With the latter two categories, but not the first, you have the opportunity of carrying out a comparative study.

Third, be clear whether you are focusing on the causes or the consequences of the phenomenon, or both. Causes precede a phenomenon, consequences follow. If your focus wanders, you are likely to find yourself in difficulty.

Fourth, if you want to 'explain' the phenomenon (or 'understand' it), think about what you mean by that term. Will you explain it by narrating the sequence of events that led up to it; or by identifying one or more mechanisms that were at work; or by identifying factors that, by their presence or absence, predisposed towards or against its occurrence; or, in the case of an action that someone took, by discovering what was in their mind?

A productive approach to explaining a phenomenon can be to ask 'Why?' questions about it. For example, 'Why did X happen?', 'Why did it take the form that it did?', 'Why did it happen when it did?' Note the presumption of causation here, that something *caused* X to happen, and to happen in the form that it did and when it did. Note, too, that such questions come into our minds against the background of presuppositions: that conceivably X might not have happened, that it might have taken a different form, that it might have happened at a different time. These presuppositions draw us into the realm of 'counterfactuals': *we are working with the infinity of events and combinations of events that did not happen.*

Faced with such puzzles, physical scientists and technologists behave differently from social scientists. The former do operate on the presumption of causation, in a 'tight' form – they presume that something *determined* that X would happen – but they minimize the part that presuppositions and counterfactuals can play in their thinking. They do this (a) by isolating the phenomenon, as far as possible; (b) by ensuring where possible that they can reproduce it, so they know their observations were not the result of an accident; (c) by controlling the conditions and changing only one independent variable at a time; and (d) by focusing on relating their observations to established theories about the mechanisms to be found in their subject of study. When they ask questions of the form 'Why did X happen?', they seek for *consistency* between their observations and established facts and theories. If they find the consistency they're looking for, they consider that they have explained why X happened.

The procedure is very similar if they start by asking open-ended questions of the form 'What will happen if ...?': they conduct an experiment to see what X results, and then seek to explain it in the same way. Or, using theory, they consciously make predictions – 'If we do V, X should happen' – and then see whether or not their predictions are fulfilled: if they are, the experimenters have attained the consistency and thus the explanation they are looking for.

In short, by taking consistency between observations and established facts and theories as the acid test of 'explanation', and by adopting a methodology in which counterfactuals play little or no part, they make their task a manageable one.

In the humanities and social sciences, explanation is much more difficult. Mostly, phenomena cannot be isolated; exact reproducibility is very difficult or impossible to attain; it is difficult or impossible to control conditions; and theories as to the mechanisms at work are, in many fields, primitive. This last point is crucial. As a student, you may well find that you are asked 'Why?' questions, which implicitly call for an explanation, but you are not offered any concept of 'explanation', or given any criterion for judging whether an 'explanation' offered to you is a good one or not. (If any criterion at all is made explicit, it is likely to be 'plausibility' rather than consistency.) Your teachers draw your attention to 'factors' that may have had a causal effect, but not to the mechanisms by which these factors operate. You are likely to be asked counterfactual questions – for example, 'Why did

China not industrialize earlier than it did?' – but not taught how to deal with such questions. In attempting to answer them you find yourself speculating about might-have-beens, and it is very easy for experienced academics to pick holes in your work.

While it cannot be disputed that social, political, economic and cultural phenomena are almost always the outcome of a complicated set of situational factors and mechanisms, and that it is much more difficult to conduct controlled experiments, the physical sciences do offer some lessons to any humanities or social science student who wants to investigate, describe and explain a phenomenon. Here are some suggestions.

- Try, as far as possible, to avoid counterfactuals in any form. Try not to make conjectures about 'might-have-beens'. Aim to make comparative studies of phenomena, so you are dealing with sets of concrete observations. Two case studies will generally be superior to one for that reason, but, as I noted earlier, because of time constraints and the word limit on your dissertation you may not be able to go into so much depth with two as you can with one. And if you are thinking about undertaking three case studies, take into account the further reduction in depth you will have to accept.

- Keep your study as simple as possible. Resist the temptation, to which many students succumb, to enquire into 'causes and consequences'. Causes will usually give you quite enough to keep you occupied. Consequences take you into the realm of counterfactuals, because you are comparing what did happen after the event (say) with what might have occurred if the event had not happened.

- If it's feasible, use several investigative methods in conjunction with one another. If you are carrying out a large-scale data-collection survey, complement it with a smaller, focused interview survey to give yourself deeper insights into the phenomenon you are investigating. If you are using one technique that reveals a correlation between two variables, use another to investigate possible cause-and-effect connections. It can be very rewarding to use in conjunction the tools of economics, sociology, psychology, geography and/or political science to investigate a behavioural phenomenon, but you *must* check that your supervisor is happy about this.

- If you are aiming to explain a phenomenon, it is bad practice to ignore any potentially relevant theory or facts. Don't impose any arbitrary exclusions or limits.

- If you are thinking about cause-and-effect relationships in terms of causal factors, try to distinguish between factors of different kinds. For example, you may be able to identify: (a) 'triggering' factors that precipitated a sequence of events; (b) factors that promoted an event and factors that enabled it; (c) 'necessary' and/or 'sufficient' conditions for an event to have occurred ('necessary' implies that in the absence of the condition the event could not have occurred; 'sufficient' implies that if the condition had been present no other conditions needed to be present for the event to occur); and/or (d) considerations of motivation, opportunity and resources that entered into the rationale behind certain decisions.

- Whatever the phenomenon that you are working on, think about mechanisms. Ask yourself what mechanisms are at work and do your best to uncover them.

- While you should do what you can to be objective – don't ask leading questions when you're interviewing people, don't make your mind up about anything before you've considered all the evidence – you should feel encouraged to question received wisdom. Arguably, objectivity is nothing more than what you get when subjectivities all agree with one another.

Investigating a phenomenon in which you are personally involved

If you are doing the kind of project that comes under the heading of participant observation, action research or qualitative research,[5] explanation will be only one of your objectives. If your aim is to change behaviour, or to intervene in or engage with an educational or political process, say, you will of course need to have some understanding of the behaviour and the process if you are to succeed in attaining your objective. The same applies even if your aim is more modest, e.g. to do no more than explore the possibilities of changing behaviour or intervening in a process.

You will almost certainly be undertaking a single case study, and in your dissertation you will need to show the examiners that you are familiar with broadly comparable case studies that others have carried out and reported in the literature; have learned and acted on practical lessons from these case studies; have meticulously recorded events and observations; have shown sensitivity to your human subjects and abided by ethical guidelines; have demonstrated skill in getting inside the minds of the people with whom you were working; have shown awareness of generalizations and hypotheses that others have produced, and asked whether they apply in your case; have yourself sought to produce generalizations and hypotheses on the basis of your observations and experience; and have reflected on your experience.

Even if you have no intention of acting as a 'change agent', if you are conducting an empirical study with human subjects there is the possibility of an 'observer effect' – the effect that you yourself have on your subjects – and you need to be aware of this and take appropriate precautions.

Testing a theory

Theories – and I include in that category theoretical models, conceptual frameworks, generalization and certain kinds of hypothesis – exist in people's minds. They are abstractions that we invent and apply when we try to make sense of what we read or hear about, or of our own first-hand experiences. For example, when we observe in the 'real world' a regularity or a pattern, we may theorize that there is an underlying cause or mechanism at work to produce it, and that it is the same one operating in all cases. If we perceive a departure from a regularity or pattern, then we reason that either the mechanism is not as we first thought, or that a particular circumstance or condition is different from those applying to the regular cases.

Although the distinction between what is in people's minds and what happens in the real world is an obvious one, in practice they readily get confused, because once we go beyond actual perceptions (empirical evidence) we can only talk in terms of concepts, mental constructs, as manifested in the language at our disposal. Hence the tendency to regard 'social class' as an intrinsic attribute of a society, whereas it is a mental construct: 'the label' becomes confused with 'the thing'. Similarly with physical phenomena: we have to use our term 'gravity' to describe the force at work when an apple removes itself from a tree to the ground.

Someone who puts forward a theory is in effect making a claim. Specifically, they are claiming that the theory is consistent with empirical observations, and possibly with other theories, too. So it is open to you to test the validity of that claim. A theory makes a suitable subject for a project if you are able to test it (your supervisor might say 'evaluate it') in some way. Before testing it, you must have a clear and precise statement of it. Once you have that, there are two main possibilities for testing: empirical testing and inspection.

Empirical testing is carried out by making observations in the 'real world'. You should aim to make observations that would help you to answer the following questions:

- Is this theory consistent with other observations that I have already made or 'facts' that I am aware of? If not, either the theory fails the test or the observations/'facts' are not to be relied on.

- Does this theory help me to make sense of my observations of a situation?

- Does this theory, which was originally formulated and found to hold in a particular set of real-world circumstances (conditions), hold in others? If you find that it doesn't, will you be able to elaborate or qualify the theory in some way to make it 'fit'?

- If this theory is valid, what can I predict, and how will I know whether the prediction is accurate? The acid test of an hypothesis is whether it enables predictions to be made and checked against reality. If the prediction is not fulfilled, the hypothesis fails: it is not valid (tenable).

Inspection can be carried out without leaving your desk. For example, you can ask the following questions:

- Is this theory internally consistent, i.e. free from internal contra-dictions? If not, the theory is unsound.

- Is this theory consistent with the observations that were made use of in developing it? Again, if not, the theory is unsound.

- Are the assumptions on which this theory is said to be based valid ones? If not, either the theory is unsound or its soundness does not actually depend on those assumptions being valid.

- Is this theory consistent with other theories? If not, either the theory or one or more of the other theories is unsound.

- Are concepts defined with sufficient precision? Do you encounter ambiguities when you try to apply definitions? Does a definition of X enable you to recognize X when you see it?

Beware theories that lack substance. Theories that have some 'meat' to them and are worth studying are almost always about relationships between variables. But there are some that don't, such as hypotheses that amount to nothing more than conjectures. You can test the hypothesis that it will rain tomorrow, but if there is no theoretical underpinning – no statement of *why* it should rain tomorrow – you learn nothing useful by awaiting tomorrow and seeing whether the hypothesis is borne out or not.

As a general rule, when setting out to test a theory, it is always worth asking the 'So what?' question about possible outcomes. Even a null result may tell you something, but if your answer to 'So what?' is 'I don't know', you need to do more thinking about your research design.

Testing a proposition or philosophical argument

To test a proposition, P, or a philosophical argument, you must first of all have a clear statement of the proposition or argument. Once you have this, and before you do anything else, unpick it: break it down into its component parts. If you are dealing with an argument, make a list of the steps in the chain of reasoning.

As in the case of testing a theory, there are a number of questions that you can use as starting points. For example:

- On what axioms, postulates or suppositions does P rest? Can these be regarded as valid? If not, P is not valid.

- Is each step in the chain of reasoning logically sound? If not, the argument is faulty.

- If P is accepted as valid ('true'), what consequences follow logically from that? Investigating these consequences can lead you into interesting territory.

Evaluating a proposal

Evaluating a proposal for a design, policy or action requires you to form and present a judgment. This has to be a three-stage process. You must ask yourself the following questions:

1. What will be the outcomes of implementing the proposal, of putting it into practice?

2. What criteria should I use for evaluation purposes? (Whenever you see the word 'evaluation', think 'criteria'!)

3. How do I apply those criteria to the outcomes I have identified?

Let's take these one by one.

The outcomes of implementing the proposal

Essentially there are three possible methods that you can use: investigation, simulation and extrapolation.

Investigation involves actually putting the proposal into practice – acting on it, implementing it – or trying it out, perhaps on a small scale, as a pilot study or trial run. In some cases, the very act of implementing it may have outcomes, and you need to be alert to these. Once the proposal has been implemented, you'll have to look for both direct outcomes, the direct 'impact' of the action or technique, and indirect, consequential outcomes, 'repercussions'.

Simulation involves constructing a model in which a proposal can be tried out. This could be a mathematical model, a computerized model, a physical small-scale model – indeed, an analogue of any kind. Whichever you use, it has to be as representative – as lifelike – as possible. Once it is up and running, you examine it to see what the outcomes will be.

Extrapolation amounts to making an informed guess about the future on the basis of the past. So you might project current trends into the future, or extrapolate from past experience of implementing a similar proposal elsewhere: in another town, say, or under another political system.

If you are a physical scientist or engineer, you will be able to depend on your knowledge of the mechanisms that operate. If you are a social scientist, whichever of these three methods you use you will inevitably encounter the counterfactual problem both in imagining what will happen following implementation and in imagining what would happen if implementation did not take place – the do-nothing scenario – as you must do if you are taking the latter as your 'benchmark' for ascertaining effects. You will often also have to face up to the possibility that whatever 'effects' you identify may be the product not only of the implemented proposal but also of other factors, and find ways of taking this into account.

What criteria to use

The criteria that you use to evaluate a design can be of two different kinds. They can be based on the designers' brief, e.g. the extent to which the objectives set out in the brief were met. So you have a question: To what extent are those objectives likely to be met? (Will it do the job? Will it sell?) Or the criteria can be 'independent' ones, such as efficiency and fairness, which you apply to the anticipated effects of the design. So you would ask: How efficient is the design likely to be when implemented? How fairly would the impact be distributed among the people affected by it?

Applying the criteria

The task you have here is to 'operationalize' your independent criteria, so you will be able to recognize and measure efficiency and fairness (say). In the latter case, that will almost certainly require you to distinguish different groups within the population, ascertain the likely costs and benefits that will fall to members of those groups, and then make your value judgments. These can only be based on your own feelings. For example, should the greatest benefit-to-cost ratio be experienced by those whose 'need' is greatest, or those who 'deserve' most, or those who will appreciate it most, or those who will be inspired to do more to help themselves? Should the needs of future generations take priority over the needs of present ones? Only you can decide. Note, however, that you are highly unlikely to be marked on your decision: it will be your working up to that point that will gain you marks.

Exploring and resolving an issue or problem

An issue, often formulated as a 'how to ...?' or 'what should be done?' question, invariably precedes proposals and actions. Issues arise in many different fields, and the language you use and approach you take will vary accordingly. For example, in engineering an issue will be treated as a 'problem', to which a 'solution' has to be found. In social/ public policy, a 'way forward' has to be found for which support can be mobilized.

But across very different fields there are common factors. Here are questions that you can ask about them:

- What is the imperative to take action? Why is it that 'something must be done'? Sometimes a problem has been badly formulated, and the 'real' problem not understood. Sometimes it is more important to be seen to be doing something than to actually do it.

- What are the objectives that action is intended to achieve? How specific are they? You may find that stated objectives are unclear and/or that there is no agreement on them. To solve a problem yourself you must be clear about your objectives.

- What constraints are there (technological, financial, political, etc.) that limit the range of actions available? Could there be an interplay, perhaps leading to compromise, between objectives and constraints, with objectives being relaxed if constraints make it impossible to achieve them, and constraints being relaxed if a high priority is attached to achieving the objectives? Again, to solve a problem yourself you must be clear about the constraints that apply and whether constraints and/or objectives can be relaxed if necessary.

- What is the history of the issue? Issues invariably have a history, a background. Investments have already been made, positions taken up. There is an inevitable reluctance to write off investment and to retreat from a position.

- What is the context of the issue? Invariably issues are connected to other issues, and whatever decision is taken will have repercussions beyond that particular issue. It will affect how those other issues are handled and probably give rise to further issues, frequently unanticipated ones.

- Who are the 'stakeholders'? These may be technical people, managers, accountants, officials, politicians and consumers – people 'on the receiving end'. Different stakeholders have their own special interests and are likely to perceive the issue differently.

- By what process can the issue be explored and resolved? This could be a purely technical, information-based 'rational' process, and/or an administrative process of going through a prescribed procedure, and/or a political process in which many stakeholders participate. Whichever is the case, and whatever your discipline, make every effort to list the steps involved in finding a (re)solution.

A project that involves exploring and resolving an issue allows you to gather information about all these aspects: perceptions of the need and scope for action, history and context, process and participants. You can use a wide variety of sources, notably documentary and people whom you can interview. You will find yourself collecting the pieces of a giant jigsaw puzzle and assembling them into the big picture. This is detective work par excellence. If you can do this systematically – step by step – it will be much easier to stand back and monitor your progress. You will need to do this if the puzzle is not to get out of hand, and you get so engrossed that you overrun your time allowance and leave yourself insufficient time to write up.

Making a critique of a creative work

Subjecting a creative work to a critique implies that you will be 'interrogating' it, taking a questioning, analytical approach to it. Your taught courses should equip you with the necessary conceptual framework and techniques for doing this, e.g. for 'deconstructing' it (or 'reading between the lines', as it used to be called). You may also be making explicit your emotional reactions to it, and analysing those too. As ever, be systematic in your approach, so: (a) identify the steps in your working; (b) list the questions you are asking; and (c) if making the critique involves you in applying certain criteria, make these explicit.

Discussing a theme

A theme invites you to identify the literature relating to it, to read the relevant parts of that literature, and to form views on it. Later on, when writing up your work, you will present your views in your dissertation.

Here are some general questions you should ask when tackling a theme:

- Does my theme have some intrinsic interest for me and for the readers of my dissertation? A theme that has intrinsic interest will help to keep you motivated and capture the attention of your readers. Disagreements (debates, challenges, controversies, contradictions and inconsistencies) provide more intrinsic interest than agreements do. Themes relating to changes over time (developments, evolution, innovation, continuities, discontinuities) have more intrinsic interest than themes relating to static conditions.

- Have I some inkling about the conclusions I might come to? Even sketchy, tentative ideas will help to give your work some direction and prevent your dissertation from becoming merely a string of unconnected points.

- Is my theme a manageable one? If the bibliography you are constructing has reached 100 or so publications and is still growing, then almost certainly your theme is too broad. Stop what you are doing and find a way of narrowing it down.

- Have I mastered the language of the subject? Unless you are really, really fluent in the academic-speak to be found in the literature you are using, you will be floundering. You will find it very difficult to

10

Project: materials

Materials and sources

Undertaking a dissertation project on your subject involves applying your brain to something. That something is 'materials' that relate to your subject. Materials are to be found in 'sources'. Broadly speaking, sources of materials fall into six categories:

- Academic literature: publications by academics and other scholars (the literature that you will already have been exploring).

- 'Subject literature': writings – whether books, plays or poetry – that are your subject of study. Books can of course be non-fiction (such as philosophical writings) or fiction.

- Professional literature: in particular, articles published in monthly and weekly journals catering for practitioners in the relevant vocational fields.

- Formal publications, such as statutes (acts of Parliament); law reports; the annual reports of government departments, other official bodies and non-governmental organizations; company reports and accounts; the published proceedings of Parliament and parliamentary committees.

- Data sources, such as census reports and published statistics of economic activity, and reference handbooks in which formulae and physical constants, for example, can be looked up.

- Ephemera: newspaper and magazine articles; and manifestations in performance media, such as film, theatre, music media, TV and radio.

Use your library

Follow the advice given on pages 28–29 for tracking down academic publications in your library and others. If your library doesn't carry much in the way of professional literature, formal publications, data sources or ephemera, it will be well worth making an effort to gain access to professional or specialist libraries that do carry these.

Use the internet

Taking advantage of your library's specialized search resources is certain to entail considerable use of the internet. Some academics discourage use of general search engines such as Google. However, Google lends itself to serendipity – the art of happy discovery by chance – especially if you can be creative in thinking of words to type in to reduce the number of web pages to a manageable few. Search engines and Wikipedia can throw up useful leads to follow, but you must always follow those leads to the original sources. Never rely on, and thus avoid the need to cite in your dissertation, an article on Wikipedia.

The internet is also the place to go to for authentic information of other kinds. For example, if you want to know how the World Trade Organization (WTO) is structured and what its formal decision-making processes are, do yourself a favour and make your first port of call not an academic textbook but the organization's website. Google > "world trade organization" < and you'll find the WTO's website at or close to the top of the list of web pages.

Extract knowledge from materials

When you have your materials in front of you, it is really important that you don't just take them at face value, that you don't regard them as unassailable, cast-iron 'knowledge'. Instead, say to yourself: 'These are the materials available, but having read them, *what do I actually know?*' In other words, having first extracted materials from publications, you now have the further task of extracting knowledge from those materials. In the right-hand column of Table 3 is shown what you can reasonably infer from materials of various kinds: their 'knowledge content'.

Table 3   The 'knowledge content' of materials

Materials	What you actually know
ACADEMIC LITERATURE	
■ Case studies, research reports and other materials ('evidence') gained from empirical investigations. These usually include not only the findings of the studies but also inferences and interpretations made by their authors.	■ That decisions were made as to what data to collect and how to collect them, and that these decisions were based on someone's judgment and preconceptions. Inferences and interpretations will be similarly subjective. What you know is nothing more than that 'So-and-so reported … and concluded …'.
■ Published theories and hypotheses typically aimed at 'explaining' or 'making sense of' observations, making predictions and/or unifying theories already in existence; writings that qualify or elaborate existing theories and hypotheses.	■ That these publications exist – their existence is a matter of public record – and that they are 'owned' by their authors, who may have strongly proprietorial feelings about them and a vested interest in getting them accepted by others. They are to be tested rather than accepted unquestioningly. Try them out to see if they are useful.
■ Published thematic material, such as reviews, commentary, critiques and argument.	■ That these publications exist, that someone had an interest in getting his or her work published, that someone or some organization considered it worth publishing and had an interest in publishing it. Accord these publications the status of 'So-and-so's opinion' and 'contributions to the current debate', to be questioned rather than taken as 'the truth'. Treat them also as potential sources of insights and ideas.

(Continued)

Table 3   The 'knowledge content' of materials *(Continued)*

Materials	What you actually know
ACADEMIC LITERATURE *(Continued)*	
■ Materials advocating or justifying a course of action.	■ That these materials were created and deployed in order to influence decisions in a way that would benefit the interests of the advocates (i.e. they would stand to gain from the outcome) and/ or advance the values to which they subscribe. Accord them the status of 'political documents', and treat them not only as rationally worked-out solutions to problems but also as the products of interests. Look out for omissions – information left out, especially if it seems to have been left out deliberately – and try to identify the values and interests that underlie them.
'SUBJECT LITERATURE' that is actually your subject of study	
■ Primary materials, ranging from 'classics' to recent and contemporary works; fiction and non-fiction; prose and poetry.	■ That you are expected to be familiar with such works (which are to be found not only in literature but also in philosophy, social psychology, sociology, economics, history, law and politics).
■ Secondary materials: works of criticism, analysis and review. (Some of these may be 'classics', too.)	■ You are also expected to be familiar with these.
PROFESSIONAL LITERATURE, especially articles published in professional journals	Articles published in professional journals are usually based on first-hand experience, the 'grass-roots' experience of participant observers in the 'real world'. As such, they must be treated as subjective – 'users' often have a set of perceptions very different from those of designers or providers – but they may provide factual information that is valuable because it comes from the real world.
FORMAL PUBLICATIONS	All of these can be taken as phenomena in their own right: their wording and their status constitute attributes of which you have unambiguous evidence. As in the case of other phenomena, you can attempt to explain why they took the form they did, why they came about when they did, etc.

Materials	What you actually know
FORMAL PUBLICATIONS *(Continued)*	
■ Statutes (acts of Parliament), secondary legislation, treaties, European regulations, law reports.	■ Students of law, public policy, international relations, etc., can take these as premises on which to base legal arguments or to develop solutions to legal problems.
■ Annual reports of government departments, other official bodies and non-governmental organizations; company reports and accounts; the published proceedings of parliament and parliamentary committees.	■ You can regard all of these as public utterances, written (or spoken) with one or more particular audiences in mind. While some spoken utterances may be involuntary (they just pop out!), others are likely to be the product of drafting and redrafting, so treat them as the output from a decision-taking process. What they do not say – i.e. what they leave out – can be as significant as, or more significant than, what they do say. Consequently they offer scope for the detective work of reading between the lines.
DATA SOURCES, such as	
■ Census reports and published statistics of economic activity.	■ That someone or some organization has reported these data in this form, *not* that this was the actuality. Some events and activities may have failed to be reported, or may have been placed in the wrong category; figures and descriptions may have been exaggerated to serve the reporter's purpose or skewed by errors of observation. Census data, for example, are well known to suffer from errors arising from the failure to count some people.
■ Reference handbooks in which formulae and physical constants, for example, can be looked up.	■ You can almost certainly treat these as givens (i.e. as factual). Don't forget to cite your sources.
EPHEMERA, such as	
■ Articles and reports in newspapers and magazines, blogs.	■ That published editions of these works exist. There may exist different editions of such works, amendments may have been made to the author's work in the course of publication, and there may be uncertainty as to who the author was.
■ Performances in or transmitted by media such as film, theatre, music, TV and radio.	■ You will usually know for certain that performances were held, but different participants, viewers and listeners may have very different perceptions of what took place.

Having reviewed the relevant materials, write yourself a note to clarify for yourself what you know at this stage. List each item separately, and be sure to include a full reference to the source of each item, to help you when you come to write your literature review and compile your list of references.

11

Project and dissertation: time management and planning

Resources

One of the most crucial resources available to you is your time. Strictly speaking, time can't be managed: it flows on and on, at the rate of 24 hours a day, seven days a week. What you have to do is make best use of the time you have got.

It's important to make a realistic assessment of the amount of time that you'll be able to put in to your project and dissertation. There are 168 hours in a week. Take away the time you need for sleeping, eating and other elements of daily living, and see what you have left. Twelve hours a day, perhaps?

Now think about the other demands on your time. Will you have to work on your project and dissertation at the same time as you are following taught courses: attending lectures; preparing for seminars, classes or tutorials; writing essays; doing laboratory work or fieldwork? These will be competing with the dissertation for your time. Most students find it very difficult to achieve a balance between these demands and the demands of their dissertation, because of their very different timescales. There's a kind of Gresham's law in operation: short-term deadlines drive out long-term ones. You find yourself giving priority to the assignment that you have to hand in next week over the one you have to hand in one or two months' time. Then all of a sudden you find that your dissertation deadline is looming: panic stations!

Clearly 'rationing by deadline' is not a good strategy in these circumstances. You need a longer-term view. You need to plan. Even if you have the summer vacation to give your dissertation work your undivided attention, you still need to plan.

Another resource that you will need to consider is your supervisor. If he or she is available for you to consult, that will be within certain windows of opportunity: they won't be continuously 'on tap', and it is highly unlikely that they will be available during vacations. So you need to plan ahead for meetings, and for anything that you submit in writing to be read, commented on and returned to you.

Plan your work

Planning your programme of work involves two things:

- Looking ahead, envisaging the tasks that you will be undertaking over the next few weeks or months, both in undertaking your project and in writing it up; and

- Taking decisions – selecting a course of action and committing yourself to it.

Bear in mind that it is virtually impossible to draw up a work programme when you start on a dissertation and not find yourself making changes to it as you learn more about your subject. Plans crystallize, dissolve and then crystallize again. At one moment you can see clearly what you should do next, then that vision fades from view and you're saying to yourself 'Hang on! Where am I going?' before arriving at a re-formed vision. To take a concrete example, you might start off with the intention of writing a dissertation on the question 'Why did Bismarck resign his post as Imperial Chancellor in 1890?' and end up writing it on 'How is it that historians can disagree so widely about the explanation of a particular event?'.

So what should you do? I suggest that you do need a plan, but it has to be flexible: it has to allow for unforeseen contingencies and for adaptation. As you learn more about your subject your objective may change, new opportunities may open up, the limitations of your resources may become apparent.

Here are some suggestions to do with planning your work:

- Construct a 'dissertation calendar' for yourself. It should show the dates and days of the week between now and your deadline, 'hand-in' day. It should also show all events that will make a demand on your time. Stick your calendar up on the wall. It's important that you keep one eye on your calendar all the time.

- Set yourself a 'comfort deadline'. Aim to complete your dissertation at least a week – preferably more – before your actual deadline. This will make it easier to accommodate unforeseen contingencies, especially setbacks. If you don't have any setbacks, and do actually meet your comfort deadline, it will allow you to put the dissertation to one side for a few days and then come back to it and read it through with a fresh eye before handing it in – always a good thing to do.

- Make a 'to do' list of the tasks that you will have to carry out, and estimate the time that each will take. For a study that entails field interviews, it might look something like that shown in Table 4.

Table 4 A typical 'to do' list with time estimates

A Carry out internet search on subject of study: 1 day
B Draw up list of relevant books and articles on subject: 2 days
C Scan literature to identify researchable subjects: 5 days
D Produce initial shortlist of research questions: 4 days
E Develop alternative titles to show supervisor: 7 days
F Consult textbooks on survey research methods: 2 days
G Produce preliminary draft of questionnaire: 2 days
H Redraft questionnaire: 1 day
I Pilot questionnaire and revise if necessary: 7 days
J Carry out 100 questionnaire-based interviews: 14 days
K Transcribe quantitative data from interviews: 4 days
L Collate qualitative data from interviews: 8 days
M Analyse data, formulate findings and think about their significance: 7 days
N Check findings against literature on subject: 3 days
O Produce preliminary draft of literature review: 3 days
P Produce preliminary draft of Discussion chapter: 6 days
Q Produce preliminary drafts of Introduction and Conclusions: 4 days
R Produce complete first draft of dissertation: 5 days
S Produce final version of dissertation: 5 days.

Add these times together. In the example in Table 4 the total is 90 days – and that makes no allowance for a spare week at the end before handing in or for any time off. If you have only two months to work on your dissertation, and plan to undertake the activities one after the other, you're in trouble. What to do?

The first thing to do is to see: (a) which activities offer scope for compressing; (b) which activities can be carried out in parallel with others; and (c) which ones can't be started until preceding ones have been completed. In the example in Table 4, you might be able to carry out C, D and E simultaneously, in five days rather than the seven that you initially allocated. Activities F–N have to be carried out in series (consecutively), but you might feel that you can't afford seven days for activity I, and that its budget has to be reduced to three. Now you've reduced the 90 days to 75.

At this point you might well feel that although it would be ideal to do 100 interviews, you simply haven't the time, and you will have to be content with 70. This will also reduce the time needed for K, L and M. You might also feel that you have to restrict the amount of qualitative data that you will collect and analyse. By this means you could bring J down to ten days and the series K–L–M to 14. The 90 days are now down to 66.

Where can you make further savings? Some ingenuity is needed here. Consider making rough notes for your Introduction, Discussion and Conclusions sections from the very beginning. If you have these notes to help you, you might be able to reduce P, Q and R to four, three and four days respectively, saving a further four days. Your total requirement now is 62 days.

If your target is 60 days, you could achieve that by allowing only three days for S, producing your final version. You don't need me to tell you that this is cutting things rather fine. Your comfort zone has almost disappeared. Your options now, it seems to me, are to reduce your interviews to 50 or even 40, or – better – to *start sooner!*

Doing for yourself an exercise like this will bring home to you the value of starting to think about and do preliminary work on your dissertation early. The earlier in the academic year that you make a start, the better. There'll be less chance that you'll get flustered, you'll have more opportunity to talk to potential supervisors, and you'll be more likely to get the supervisor you want.

Produce your first outline

Now write another note to yourself. Draw up a tentative outline, version01, for your dissertation as soon as you can. (An outline, or plan, consists of the headings and subheadings you will use.) Something simple like the sample shown in Table 5 will be sufficient at this stage.

Table 5   First attempt at dissertation outline

1. Introduction
      Why topic is an interesting one
      Central question (research question)
      Methodology
      Materials
      Outline of following chapters
2. Literature review
3. Work done
4. Findings
5. Discussion
6. Conclusions

Your first attempt at a dissertation outline is provisional. Soon you'll review it and find you want to flesh it out and modify it. Dissertation outlines *always* undergo change. It is helpful to have a draft outline from early in the process, but you could easily go through a dozen or more versions before arriving at the final one. As I say, this is normal: don't be discouraged if you find it happening to you. It shows that you are being flexible, not that you are producing a series of faulty outlines.

Part 3
The 'middle period'

12

Keeping everything under control

You can think of the 'middle period' of producing a dissertation as beginning when you've decided on your subject and approach and get down to serious work, and ending when you move into 'writing up' mode.

The middle period can be a scary time. You can't yet see your dissertation taking shape, so you need to have faith that things will turn out all right. You may come across new publications that demand to be read, and find you've lost days while you were reading them. You may find you've opened up several lines of enquiry, and your project is opening out, 'diverging' rather than 'converging'. If you're doing practical work, you may find you're getting results that you didn't expect and have to reorganize your thoughts to take them on board. Early on it may feel as though you've got plenty of time to do the work – then all of a sudden you realize that the deadline is uncomfortably close. At some point, you may find yourself thinking 'Have I taken on too much?' And, if you're anything like most other people in this situation, you are liable to find your emotions going up and down. All this can contribute to making you feel tense and pressurized. While a bit of pressure can generate adrenaline and energize you, too much pressure plus uncertainty will generate anxiety – probably not a state of mind in which you think clearly and do your best work.

In short, you need to take charge of events. Fortunately there are a number of practical things you can do. You can take on the role of 'managing' yourself, you can get going on your literature review, and you can keep your dissertation outline under review. These are the subjects of the next few chapters of this book.

13

Project: being your own manager

Being your own manager means monitoring your progress, looking ahead to your conclusions, and managing your thought processes. I deal with these in turn.

Monitor your progress

Check with your dissertation calendar every day or two to see whether you're on schedule, ahead of schedule or slipping behind. It is of course especially important to know if you're slipping behind, so you can either take steps to catch up or adjust the calendar.

Be aware of what you're doing in the here-and-now, especially if you have come up against a problem. In that situation, it is very easy to get sidetracked into displacement activities, such as 'binge reading'. At such times, stop, take stock, and address the problem. It may be that you need to take a day off and do something restful and/ or recreational. (The back of your mind will carry on working even when the front is occupied with an activity, so you will probably lose less time than you think.)

Notice, too, when you are trying to do too many things at once. If you have a sense of things getting out of control, you need to detach yourself from the day-to-day and take some decisions about your work programme: what to continue with and what to cut. Even if cutting means writing off some of the time and effort you have invested in your project, don't hesitate. There are times when you must be ruthless!

Look ahead to your conclusions

As soon as you enter the middle period, start looking ahead to the conclusions of your project. Doing this keeps your goal in front of you.

It's OK to make tentative guesses as to what your conclusions might be. (I emphasize the 'tentative' – you must be open to the possibility of arriving at different conclusions.) If you don't look ahead, you are in effect going on a journey without even the vaguest of maps.

Remember that your conclusions can be of three kinds:

■ Your conclusions about the subject – if you are starting off from a question, your conclusions must incorporate your answer(s) to the question.

■ A critique of the literature informed by the work you have done.

■ Your reflections on your methodology, including any problems or ethical issues that you encountered.

Ideally you will write something about each of these in the Discussion and/or Conclusions chapters of your dissertation. So start making notes on them now. At this stage these will be notes for your eyes only, part of your 'writing as thinking' process, so don't worry about polishing them for other people to see.

Manage your thought processes

Thinking is an inherently untidy process. Our thoughts go to and fro, ideas and questions pop into our heads, we turn over the day's events in our minds, we think laterally and we think about future possibilities. We digest what we have seen or heard or read, we try to make sense of apparent inconsistencies. Out of this messy process we have to produce a dissertation that is essentially linear, that takes the reader through a logical progression from Introduction to Conclusions. That's quite a challenge! Here are some ideas on how to rise to it:

■ If your head is always full of stuff, or if your mind 'races', write down your thoughts as they come to you. It will free up your brain. Likewise, when new questions occur to you and possible answers come into your mind, or when you come across some interesting reading, write a note to yourself about it. Writing things down will contribute hugely to clarifying your thoughts.

■ Take every opportunity that arises to talk to other people about your project and dissertation. They don't have to be experts in the subject, and sometimes it's better if they're not. The point is not so much to get feedback – although feedback may be useful – as to make yourself articulate your thoughts. You'll find that talking about your work clarifies it in your mind; and since the whole of your dissertation amounts to an articulation of your thoughts, the more practice you can get at doing this, the better.

- If there's no one else around to talk to, feel free to talk to yourself. It's not a sign of madness, simply a way of slowing your mind down. Even if you're a fast talker, your talking speed will almost certainly be significantly slower than your thinking speed.

- Write notes to yourself as you go along, on your methodology (e.g. on practical difficulties that have arisen in applying it), on materials that you are using (e.g. on the reliability of sources), on your findings and their significance, and so on. Some of these notes you will discard later, but others will be prototypes of the building blocks out of which you will construct your dissertation. It's 'writing as thinking' again.

Manage the practicalities of writing

As with any project that involves writing and the use of computers, there will be practical hazards to contend with. Computer crashes and loss of work will earn you commiseration and sympathy but nothing else. Here are some suggestions:

- Back up your work frequently and put your back-up copy somewhere safe!. This is absolutely crucial. If you're going to be paranoid about anything, be paranoid about losing your work. Save it on your institution's server, put it on a memory stick, open a gmail account and email it to yourself at your gmail address. If you're working on your own PC, you *must* put back-up copies elsewhere.

- At the start of every day that you work on your dissertation, create a fresh copy of your work and begin from that. Open the latest version of your draft, alter the file name from v21 to v22, or whatever, save it, then open it. If you ever feel that you have gone down the wrong path, you'll be able to go back to an earlier version and start again.

- Save your work every time you stop to think. Get used to doing this automatically.

- Make your work easier to read, both on screen and on paper. Use a clear, decent-sized font and a line spacing greater than 1 (1.5 is a commonly used spacing; if you find it's uncomfortably big, try 1.2).

- Lift your eyes off the screen at frequent intervals.

14

Dissertation: creating your literature review

What goes in a literature review?

Except for fields where literature is your subject, it is a standard requirement for dissertations that they should incorporate a literature review. What should go in yours?

A good literature review has to be more than just a list of your sources with an abstract or summary of each one, otherwise it will give the examiners the message that you have not 'got under the skin' of the literature, that you haven't digested it, that you haven't been able to read critically. You will be fortunate if your dissertation earns a pass mark.

To write a good literature review, you must ask yourself 'What am I reviewing the literature *for*?' The answer you should get is twofold: you are reviewing the literature (a) to provide yourself with a 'platform' for your project, and (b) to provide yourself with material for the Discussion chapter of your dissertation.

While working your way towards these goals, however, you must be aware of a 'trap' that lies in wait for you.

The literature review 'trap'

Many students, when they start writing their literature review, feel they have to summarize everything that has been written on their subject. So they collect a mass of books and photocopied articles, and then sit down to write a potted summary of it all. Faced with this mass of publications, their task turns into a nightmare. They don't know where to start, they don't know how to organize their material, and when they start writing they soon find they are in danger of their review taking up far too many of the words at their disposal. Instead of heading towards 10 to 15 per cent, it's heading towards 50 per cent.

What's happening here is that their 'literature review' is turning into a review of the whole subject. It's becoming a long essay in its own right; it's taking over their dissertation. This is not what should happen.

The literature review as a 'platform' for your project

I made the point above that one of your purposes in reviewing the literature will be to provide yourself with a 'platform' for your project. This implies asking yourself 'What is there in the literature that is relevant to my project, that provides me with a starting point, something to build on?' You need to pick out – highlight – elements of the literature that you are actually going to use or refer to later.

Here are some suggestions as to the platform that your literature review can supply for your project:

- Questions. A concise, to-the-point question is a prize worth having. The literature might supply one, in a form that you can immediately use – maybe it's a question asked about one subject that can validly be asked about another – or in a form that you can adapt. Maybe the literature will suggest a question to you. And if you are asking questions that are the same as, or similar to, the questions that others have asked, there will probably be some 'mileage' – some value – in comparing the answers you get with the answers that they arrived at.

- Descriptions of phenomena, especially in case study form, as might be found in research reports. You could investigate different but similar phenomena, with a view to carrying out a comparative study. You could take note of the 'dimensions' of the phenomena that the writer used (i.e. the features that he or she chose to measure and report on) and use the same ones yourself, or you might feel that the writer overlooked some significant ones, in which case you could point this out (with your reasons) and go on to work with your preferred set of dimensions. Your own study, when you have completed it, might enable you to include in your dissertation an informed critique of other people's studies.

- A summary of the current debate on a topic. Here you could highlight differences between writers, and unresolved questions, and then go on to explore these.

- An overview of the theories and associated conceptual frameworks put forward by different writers. You could highlight similarities and differences, as a precursor to testing these in terms of their internal consistency and their consistency with observations that you will be making.

- A summary of a particular writer's argument, which you then go on to test or subject to a critique.

- An overview of an issue, where you highlight different perceptions of the issue and different proposals as to what actions should be taken, before developing your own proposals.

- A list of different aspects of a theme: you can then go on to discuss, taking each aspect in turn, what there is in the literature on each, before offering your own contribution.

- A review of different methodologies, highlighting the salient features of each, before going on to apply one or more.

- Literature can also provide background to a study – a historical background, for example. Such literature, if it is only background rather than central, merits only a brief summary in your literature review.

(It may be that you need to review several kinds of literature. No problem – you simply divide your literature review into the necessary number of sections.)

A problem commonly encountered when writing a literature review is that of how extensively to quote from the material that you have read. It is very easy indeed to find yourself quoting large chunks from books and articles. As I pointed out in Chapter 5, this happens because you aren't clear exactly what will be relevant to your project, and you don't know yet what you will be referring to in the Discussion section of your dissertation. It can also happen because you're so engrossed in nitty-gritty detail at this point that you lose sight of the bigger picture, which, if you were aware of it, would reveal some details to be not very significant. As before, I suggest that you make your notes as sketchy as possible but keep your materials close at hand and well indexed, so that you can refer back to them quickly and easily.

If your subject material actually *is* literature, e.g. the classic writings of great thinkers, you will be referring to it, quoting from it and analysing it later on in your dissertation. So don't do so at length in your literature review, otherwise you'll be repeating yourself later on. Repetition uses up words, doesn't gain you any marks, and is liable to irritate the examiners. Avoid it.

There are three final points to make about compiling a literature review.

First, your coverage of the literature should be as comprehensive as you can make it. Don't run the risk of examiners saying that you have omitted to read something significant. If preparing a comprehensive literature review would require you to read hundreds of items, then almost certainly your subject is too broad – you must narrow it down – and has been 'done to death' by writers before you, leaving little or no scope for you to say anything interesting about it.

Second, some sources are academically more impressive than others when cited in a dissertation. So don't reproduce chunks of text from standard textbooks. Depending on the subject and your teachers' predilections, references to material appearing in upmarket newspapers might be acceptable – but do check! – more particularly factual records of recent events and the utterances of participants in them, and comment by reputable academics rather than columnists.

Third, and crucially important, you really, really must cite all your sources, i.e. give references for them, so that a reader could look them up for himself or herself if they wished. I spell out the reasons for doing this later on, in Chapter 21. You'll see that one of the reasons is to avoid laying yourself open to accusations of plagiarism. So you must be meticulous about recording details of every verbatim quotation (in quotation marks) that you include; of every piece of writing that you have paraphrased; and of writings, lectures etc., the content of which you have digested and drawn on.

Multidisciplinary subjects

If your subject is one that is dealt with in several discipline-based literatures ('household formation' comes up in demography, sociology, economics and social policy; 'diaspora nationalism' in anthropology and international relations), your literature review will have to draw together the particular contributions of these diverse literatures. How to do this? Here are some suggestions:

- Get clear in your mind what the phenomenon is that you are concerned with (human behaviour and utterances, events, situations or whatever) and what observations have been made of it. (In your reading, ignore journalistic opinion, commentary, punditry – ask yourself 'What do I actually *know*?') If writers from different disciplines notice different features of the phenomenon, you already have something interesting to write about.

- Master the terminology used by writers from the different disciplines, and the concepts, theories, assumptions etc. that are in their minds. Make yourself a 'dictionary' of terms, with your own translations and illustrations. Then work out how they all fit together, or not; how they complement or conflict with one another. Now identify the *questions* that writers from different disciplines ask, in their own languages, when they 'interrogate' phenomena. Now see what you get when you apply the whole multidisciplinary battery of questions. Don't forget to include in your dissertation's Discussion and Conclusions a note on the problems that you have encountered in carrying out a multidisciplinary study.

Save your critical appraisal of the literature for later

Don't forget that when you have completed your project you will be in a far better position to deliver a critical appraisal of the literature than you are in the 'middle period'. It follows that the logical place to do this is in the Discussion and Conclusions chapters of your dissertation, not in the literature review itself.

15

Project and dissertation: making use of quotations

Use quotations appropriately

In addition to serving as a platform for your project, your literature review provides you with material for the Discussion chapter of your dissertation. It provides something for you to get your teeth into. It provides you with quotations.

Students who are compiling a literature review often find themselves quoting at length from their source when they start. Later on, when they are polishing up and editing their dissertation, they return to these quotations and attempt to trim them down. This may not be an easy task, especially under last-minute pressures. So it's worth doing what you can to avoid getting into this situation.

When you find a quotation that you want to use, please scrutinize it carefully. Think about what its significance is and what you want to use it *for.* It is not enough to say 'According to X, ...' or 'X states ...', because that implies a 'neutrality' which is often absent. It will also show the reader that you have not thought sufficiently about its significance. So ask questions about it.

The contribution made by a quotation may take one of a variety of forms, each requiring to be referred to in its appropriate way. In Table 6,[6] I have listed these forms and suggested the appropriate ways to refer to them. I also offer some questions that you can ask about them to establish their significance.

You may come across a quotation that strikes you as highly significant but doesn't fit neatly under any of the headings in Table 6. In that case, just ask yourself this simple, all-purpose, knife-through-butter question about it: 'So what?'

Quotations on their own are 'raw' material – you need to 'digest' them, especially if they use the technical language of the subject or

Table 6   Using quotations appropriately

Type of contribution	How to refer to it	Questions to ask about it
Fact	X found, discovered, revealed, ascertained, notes, points out that …	Is this fact universally accepted, accurate (so far as you can tell)? Have other significant facts been ignored? How am I using this fact?
Perception	X describes, identifies, distinguishes, categorizes; as X sees it, …	Does X have a particular standpoint that causes him/her to perceive things in this particular way? Are there alternative standpoints?
Figure of speech	X regards … as; compares … to; suggests that … is like …	Is this an appropriate metaphor or simile? How does it assist my understanding? Do I want to adopt it?
Definition	X defines … to mean …	Do other writers have different definitions, i.e. attribute different meanings to the same term?
Assumption	X assumes, postulates, hypothesizes, conjectures, takes it for granted that …	Do other writers make this assumption? Is it valid, justified? Do I wish to share it? If I make different assumptions, would I come to different conclusions?
Proposition	X argues, asserts, contends, suggests, hypothesizes … that if A, then B; X supports, is critical of, criticizes …	How can I test the validity of this proposition, whether it 'fits the facts'?
Opinion	According to X; X tells us, says, thinks, suggests, considers, comments, agrees that … ; X disagrees with … ; in X's opinion; it seems to X that …	On what grounds (evidence) does X base his opinions? Do other people hold them? If not, why not? Do I agree with X?
Value judgment	To X, it should, ought; to X it is good, bad, beneficial, harmful that …	Do other people share X's value judgments? Why should I pay attention to them?
Claim	X claims that; in X's professional judgment; to X, it surely, must be, is obvious that; it cannot be; common sense dictates	What is the authority on which X bases his/her claim? Why shouldn't I challenge that claim and authority?
Question	X asks/questions whether	Are these questions relevant? Are there other questions that I ought to be asking?
Reasoning	X infers from this evidence that … ; shows from his/her analysis that … ; X demonstrates how … ; concludes	Is this reasoning sound? Could other conclusions be drawn from the same evidence?

are expressed in an authoritative voice. Digesting requires you first of all to paraphrase the quotation. 'To paraphrase' is defined in the *Oxford Dictionary of English* (2nd edition) as 'to express the meaning of [something written], using different words, especially to achieve greater clarity'. Greater clarity is precisely what you need. In effect, you have to translate the quotation into language that makes sense to you. (Don't merely substitute new words for some of the original ones, or change the order of words in a sentence: clarify!)

The second step in digesting is to 'engage' with the quotation, to 'internalize' it, so it is not only clearer to you but part of the thinking and reasoning that's going on in your own head. Asking the questions shown in the right-hand column of Table 6 will help you to do this. It is only when you have asked and answered such questions that you have comprehended a quotation's significance and can demonstrate that significance to your readers. To get to that point you must, of course, be fluent in the technical language of the quotation, not merely able to translate it with the aid of a dictionary.

If your review as you have drafted it contains lengthy quotations from the literature, almost certainly you haven't fully digested what you have read. At some point – not necessarily now – take a fresh look at those quotations, for each one ask 'So what?', and write down your answer. If your quotations consist largely of description, again shorten them as much as you can. You earn marks for showing the examiners that you can appreciate the significance of quotations, not for your ability to copy them out.

There is an important point here for master's students who have done their first degree at a university outside the UK. You may previously have been in an educational system where you were expected to be able to quote authorities and textbooks, and were rewarded for doing no more than this. At UK institutions you will find it is not the same. You are expected to *use* quotations in the way I have described above, not merely reproduce them, and to show in your essay that you have understood their relevance to the topic.

16

Dissertation: developing your outline

Keep your dissertation outline under review

As your work progresses through its middle period, you must keep the outline (plan) of your dissertation – the headings and subheadings – constantly under review, even while you are concentrating on your project. Reviewing your outline in the light of your project work will help to keep your thinking clear and focused. Often it will become apparent to you that you could improve your outline. Everyone finds their outline developing through the middle period of their work.

My first suggestion for a dissertation outline (see Table 5) was very much an all-purpose one:

1. Introduction
     Why topic is an interesting one
     Central question (research question)
     Methodology
     Materials
     Outline of following chapters

2. Literature review

3. Work done

4. Findings

5. Discussion

6. Conclusions

As you review your outline, it will become more specialized and detailed. In Table 7 are shown six general examples. Does one of them suit you? You could start from that model and adapt it by inserting headings and subheadings that are particular to your subject.

Table 7   Six general dissertation outlines

1. Investigative and comparative study using desk research
1. Introduction
    Background/context
    Research question
    Brief review of literature on the topic
    Structure of remainder of dissertation
2. Methodology
    Review of literature on methodology
    Features to be compared and method of comparing them
3. Materials
    List of materials and sources
4. Findings (observations)
5. Discussion (analysis)
    Synthesis of findings
    Significance of findings
    Critique of literature in light of findings
    Reflections on methodology and materials used
6. Conclusions
    Answer to research question, in brief
    Further implications of the study

2. Investigative and comparative study using fieldwork
1. Introduction
    Why subject is interesting
    Purpose of study (question to be answered)
    Conceptual framework (way(s) of looking at the subject)
    Structure of remainder of dissertation
2. Literature review
    Practical issues and debates
    Theoretical issues
    Published case study material (other people's fieldwork)
    Literature on methodology
3. Case study 1
    Work done
    Findings
4. Case study 2
    Work done
    Findings
5. Discussion
    Overview of findings: similarities and differences
    Interpretation of findings
    Explanation of similarities and differences
    Reflections on methodology and theory
6. Conclusions
    How purpose of study has been met, in brief
    Need for further research, in brief

---

3. Testing a theory
1. Introduction
    The place of the theory in current academic thinking
    Purpose of study: why the theory needs to be tested
        (Implied question: Is the theory valid?)
    Brief outline of methodology
    Structure of remainder of dissertation
2. Literature review
    Review of publications describing the theory
    Review of critiques of and commentary on the theory
    Review of publications setting out alternative, complementary etc. theories
3. Your description of the theory
    Foundations: origin, postulates, presumptions, etc.
    Variables, causal relationships
    What the theory predicts
4. Testing of the theory
    Against evidence: do findings corroborate predictions?
    In its own terms: internal consistency, validity of postulates, presumptions, etc.
    Against other theories: consistency
5. Discussion
    Inferences drawn from results of testing
    Validity of theory (answer to question)
    Usefulness of theory
    How theory might be improved
6. Conclusions
    Summary of discussion

---

4. Evaluative study
1. Introduction
    Context of the study
    Personal interest in the subject
    What is to be evaluated (e.g. design, policy)
    Purpose of evaluation
        (Implied question: How good is the design?)
    Methodology: criteria to be applied, and how they were chosen
    Structure of remainder of dissertation
2. Overview of the literature
    Subject material
    Evaluation studies and methodology
3. Exploration
    How design or policy would be implemented
    Likely outcomes and repercussions
4. Evaluation
    Results of applying criteria to likely outcomes, etc.

(Continued)

Table 7   Six general dissertation outlines *(Continued)*

4. Evaluative study *(Continued)*
5. Discussion
    Significance of results
    Objectivity/subjectivity problems encountered
    Quality of design (answer to question), dependence on criteria used
    Implications of findings for design and policy-making processes
    Critique of current practices
    Other lessons learned
6. Conclusions
    How good the design, policy etc. is
    Value of this study: implications for future designs, policies, etc.
    Summing up

5. Treatment of a theme
1. Introduction: the theme
    Historical background
    Overview of the literature: current issues and debate
    Aspects examined
    Methodology and materials
    Structure of remainder of dissertation
2. Aspect 1
    The literature
    Observations
    Interpretation of observations
3. Aspect 2
    The literature
    Observations
    Interpretation of observations
4. Aspect 3
    The literature
    Observations
    Interpretation of observations
5. Discussion
    Synthesis of observations and interpretations
    Overview of aspects
    Implications for current issues and debate
6. Conclusions: summary of discussion

6. Argument
1. Introduction
    Background/context
    Thesis: what is being argued
    Rival theses: why this thesis is being argued
    How the thesis is being argued: structure of remainder of dissertation

6. Argument *(Continued)*
2. The literature
    Academic literature
    Professional literature
3. Construction of thesis
    Underpinnings: axioms and presumptions
    Edifice: reasoning
    Pinnacle
4. Corroboration of thesis
    Relevant evidence: academic (theoretical and applied)
    Relevant evidence: professional (documented experiences)
5. Alternative theses: their defects
    Relevant evidence: academic (theoretical and applied)
    Relevant evidence: professional (documented experiences)
6. Discussion
    Why neutrality is not an option
    Why my thesis is the best
7. Conclusions: restatement of thesis

You can start with the outline that is closest to what you need and then modify it to suit your particular needs. As a general rule, you should try to *elicit* – to *discover* – the structure that best suits your presentation, rather than *impose* a structure on it.

As you can see, all the outlines shown in Table 7 offer you a systematic and logical structure for your dissertation. In my experience, these models work well for dissertations and examiners appreciate them, not least because the list of contents and the final section of the Introduction provide 'signposts' that are straightforward and easy to follow. And for you as a writer, it provides a convenient way of transforming messy, untidy, jumping-about thinking into what necessarily has to be a linear presentation.

Part 4
The 'end game'

17

The challenge to complete

As you enter the 'end game' of your work, seeing your deadline looming up will concentrate your mind and get your adrenaline flowing. At this point it's worth making an effort to minimize uncertainty. Uncertainty adds to your anxiety and consequently increases the pressure on you. This is something you already have enough of.

Consequently you must *plan* what you are going to do in the time remaining. This means looking ahead: checking that you have enough time for the work you think you still need to do on your project and for writing up your dissertation; and minimizing – if not eliminating – the possibility of surprises that might cause you to have an agonizing rethink.

In this part of the book, I outline the work you will have to do in the end-game stage. You can see from the chapter headings how the emphasis shifts from your project, as you complete your work on it, to your dissertation. I have subdivided work on your dissertation into a sequence of four stages: finalizing your outline and producing a first draft; improving your draft; ensuring that your dissertation conforms to good academic practice; and final editing of your dissertation.

18

Project: concluding
your work

Set a realistic 'cut-off' date for your project work

In the end-game stage, you must set a 'cut-off' date for completing your project work. This cut-off date must be realistic, in two senses. First, it must be a realistic expectation that you will actually complete your project work by that date – taking account of your recent work rate, you must judge whether it is indeed feasible to achieve that. Second, the date must be a realistic one in that it will leave you enough time before your handing-in deadline to do a good job of writing up your dissertation.

All too often, students set a cut-off date, and then overrun it. This is asking for trouble. The underlying problem may be that you don't know when to stop. Students in this position do often ask 'How do I know when I've done enough?' If you find yourself in this situation, ask a different question: 'Have I enough to say in my Discussion and Conclusions?' Almost certainly your answer to this question will help you to see how you can wind up your project work speedily.

The fact is that, whatever your project, and whatever stage you've reached, there is always more you could do. If you haven't yet got to your cut-off date, keep an eye open for 'diminishing returns', the situation in which adding a worthwhile point to your Conclusions would require a disproportionate amount of work. You can always add a short paragraph on 'further research needed' to show that you have given some thought to how your work could usefully be extended.

The eleventh-hour rethink

For me to say that you should set yourself a cut-off date and stick to it is to offer you a counsel of perfection. Quite often the unexpected does happen, and students do find themselves having an eleventh-hour rethink. It may be because they have seen an opportunity to add something brilliant, and can't resist the temptation to incorporate it in their work. At the other extreme it may be because disaster has struck – for example, they discover that there's an important book or article on their subject that they haven't read, or that they made an assumption early on that now looks as though it's not valid, or they forgot to take measurements of a variable that now looks as though it's a crucial one.

To avoid the necessity for an eleventh-hour rethink, do the following things before your cut-off date:

- Check your literature. Ask yourself: 'Is there anything I might have missed?'

- Check that you are still happy with all the assumptions you made earlier.

- Check your early results.

- Go over the notes you have written for yourself. See if there's anything that you would want to change. Check your reasoning. Look for inconsistencies and loose ends. If you come across any leads you want to follow up, make sure that it would be profitable to do so. You can't afford to get diverted down any side-tracks.

19

Dissertation: producing your first draft and finalizing your outline

When you are producing your first full draft you will almost certainly find that you want to revise the outline that you are using. This is perfectly normal. It is only when you are actually drafting chapters and sections that you come to realize that the logical place for something is not where you originally put it; or that a chapter is either too long, and needs to be split in two, or too short, and needs to be incorporated into another. Consequently, expect to keep revising your outline while you are producing your first full draft (and possibly for some time after). In effect, you develop both your outline and your first full draft until they coincide. You need to have an outline in order to start producing your draft, but as your draft develops you will almost certainly want to modify your outline. Never attempt to force the draft to fit the outline that you had in mind before you started to produce your draft.

From 'writing as thinking' to 'writing as presenting'

At the point in time when you start work on the first draft of your dissertation, you should have a collection of notes that you have already made: the products of 'writing as thinking' while you have been getting on with your project.

Writing as thinking, when you're sorting your ideas out, is usually a messy business: untidy, disjointed, spontaneous and sometimes repetitive, because you find yourself going over things again. This is why short notes are the best way of recording your thoughts. But a dissertation has to be more than a collection of short notes. It has to be 'linear' in form: chapter after chapter and paragraph after paragraph in a logical sequence that is easy for the reader to follow. Each chapter and each paragraph has only one before it and only one following it.

You must be aware, therefore, that in writing a dissertation you are not giving an account of your work, with all the false starts and twists and turns that it entailed, or even of your thoughts, which may exist in your mind as a network of connected points or as a constellation of unconnected ones. Rather, you are in the business of *presentation*: you have to assemble your dissertation to produce something that is as linear as possible for the reader to follow. So when you start drafting your dissertation you move away from 'writing as thinking' towards 'writing as presenting', although – of course – you don't stop thinking while you're writing with your reader in mind!

Create a 'linear' presentation

Turning your collection of notes into a linear presentation presents you with a challenge. What models are there to follow? The most obvious example of a linear presentation is to be found in fiction writing, in the form of the story. Here events are not merely a sequence along a 'time line': they 'unfold', with each providing the context for the next. The reader reads on, not just to find out what happens next, but with his or her mind informed by each event as they encounter it. In the realm of dissertations, the next best thing is the 'question-to-answer' format, in which you lead the reader along a logical track. Outlines 1–4 shown in Table 7 are of this kind.

The problem that you are likely to face is that the sections of your dissertation simply do not conform to a linear pattern. Here are four instances:

- You want to write a section on your methodology, a section on your materials and a section on applying your methodology to your materials. The only logical connection here is that your 'applying' section draws on both your 'methodology' and 'materials' sections. There is no logic that compels you to place 'methodology' before 'materials', or vice versa. So how do you hold your reader 'in suspense', as it were, after the first section, while you lead him or her through the second?

- You have a logical sequence of paragraphs, leading from one on to the next, each devoted to a single point. Then you decide that a paragraph in the middle of the sequence needs to have another paragraph tacked on, giving more detail, perhaps, or dealing with a point you've come across in the literature. In effect, that extra paragraph leads the reader down a side-track – how are you going to get back on to the main track?

- You are writing about a number of points 'in parallel', so to speak – a number of case studies, or several different attributes of a phenomenon, or the view from different disciplinary perspectives – and there is no logical reason for preferring any particular order. In this case, how are you going to move forwards smoothly after dealing with the last one?

- You have a 'matrix' of things that you want to write. For example, you have been carrying out a comparative study of England, France and Germany, examining (let's say) social, political and economic conditions. Do you have a chapter on each of the three countries, and subdivide each chapter into sections on social, political and economic conditions? Or do you have a chapter each on social, political and economic conditions, and subdivide each chapter into sections on each country? And, whichever you choose, how do you subsequently get back on to a single track?

The answer to all these questions lies in giving your reader 'signposts', so that he or she can grasp your structure at a glance. There are four concrete things you can do:

- Formulate your outline using subheadings in addition to main (chapter) headings. Sometimes it will be helpful to use sub-subheadings, too. In doing this you are giving your reader a detailed map, not a schematic one. The more detail, the easier it will be for readers to find their way around your dissertation. You can also group chapters together into parts if you think this would help the reader.

- When formulating your outline, put the 'side-tracks' under subheadings or sub-subheadings. Material under a subheading or sub-subheading doesn't have to lead on to material under the next main heading – the reader won't expect it to, and won't be 'thrown' when it doesn't.

- To get back on the main track after you've worked your way through several parallel points or case studies, or after a matrix of writing, where you have used subheadings, add a synthesis, review or overview. So, for example, you might end up with a sequence of four subheadings: 'Case study 1', 'Case study 2', 'Case study 3' and 'Overview of case studies'. It will be immediately apparent to the reader how you have organized your thoughts.

- Use the final section of your Introduction to tell the reader how you have organized your dissertation. Although this may amount to little more than a summary of your outline – and thus of your Contents page – it will help the reader to find his or her way around, and reassure them that you know what you're doing.

Your first draft

Your first draft need be little more than a stringing together of your notes. Certainly there will be gaps, overlaps, rough edges, discontinuities and inconsistencies. The value of your first draft is that it will reveal these to you. You can then go on to deal with them in the course of improving your draft.

It will also be well worth while, when you're working on your first draft, to keep thinking about what you are going to put in your Discussion and Conclusions. The clearer you can be about these, the surer you will be about where the dissertation is heading, and what you do and don't need to put in the earlier chapters. If you haven't yet finished your project work, doing this will also help you to be clearer about what you need to do to finish.

20

Dissertation: improving your draft

Build on your first draft

Your first draft of your dissertation will be a patchy, rough-and-ready affair. Now it's time to start improving it. You don't need to begin at the beginning and work your way through to the end: you can work on sections in any order. It's quite common for sections to 'grow up' together. But you must bear in mind that what you are doing is *improving*, knocking your dissertation into shape – you are not yet at the stage of polishing, and you should definitely not attempt to polish your dissertation until you have been through the improving stage.

Synchronize and tidy up

An important part of improving your draft is 'synchronizing' the various chapters and sections. For example, your Introduction must be 'in sync' with your Conclusions. You cannot afford to have an answer in your Conclusions that does not match a question posed in your Introduction, and this may mean changing the question!

Similarly, it is only when you have made progress with your Discussion that you will know which bits of the literature you have used are relevant to your presentation, and can tailor your literature review accordingly, deleting quotations etc. that you don't refer to later. It will be a waste of time to polish up and edit down your literature review until you know what you are going to say in your Discussion.

Tidying up means putting things in their proper place. So check that your chapters and sections are in the most logical order. If not, move them around until you find it. And gather together components that are alike. For example, when you read through your first draft you may find you've introduced new questions in your Discussion: bring them forward to join the questions in your Introduction. And do not, under any circumstances, introduce new material in your Conclusions. If you can't find an appropriate place for it in an earlier chapter, even your Discussion, there is something not right with your structure – you need to give it further thought.

Make your dissertation reader-friendly

The examiners who read your dissertation will certainly appreciate it if you have put some effort into making it reader-friendly. Here are some suggestions for achieving this:

- Know your reader. There may still be some academics around who want to see a continuous piece of prose that is not divided up into chapters and sections. Check whether your dissertation will be read by one of these. If so, you must humour them. Divide your draft into chapters and sections, but delete the headings from the final version. Leave an extra line or insert a few asterisks between the 'chapters'. You may need to incorporate the section headings (subheadings) into the first sentence of the 'section', using a form of words like 'Turning now to ...', 'With regard to ...' or 'Consideration must be given to ...'.

- Give your reader clear 'signposts'. Include a 'Contents' page, and include subheadings (section headings) as well as chapter headings. Be sure to end your Introduction with a paragraph saying how the remainder of the dissertation is organized. And begin each middle chapter with a sentence saying what you will do in that chapter.

- There is no right length for chapters, but they usually turn out to have a 'natural' length. As a rough guide I would expect your Introduction to comprise around 10 per cent of your total words and your Conclusions around 5 per cent. If you have six chapters in all, then the middle four would each comprise 15–25 per cent. If one of those middle chapters has more than 30 per cent, see if you can find a neat way of splitting it. Likewise, if one of the middle chapters has less than 10 per cent, see if you can combine it with another. For example, if there is very little that needs to be said about your methodology, have a section on it in your Introduction rather than giving it a chapter to itself.

■ Use lists where they will provide clarity, but do not use them just for the sake of it. Bullet points are probably best used sparingly, if not avoided altogether. They will impart a staccato quality to your work and this could jar with the reader.

■ Use illustrations, diagrams and tables where appropriate, and insert them into the text. (Don't group them together at the end.) A relevant illustration or diagram can make a point clearly and save you a couple of hundred words. A table can present a mass of data in a very concise form. The reader will not go through it in detail, but will want to refer to it to see if the inferences you have drawn from it are justified.

■ It may be permissible to put some factual material in appendices, at the end of the dissertation. Again, they will be there if the reader wants to refer to them. No substantive part of your dissertation should be relegated to an appendix.

■ In the interests of reader-friendliness, pay attention to presentation. Make your dissertation *look* attractive: that will make it easy to read, too. Leave white space above and below headings and paragraphs, so your writing doesn't appear 'cramped'. If you have any choice in the matter, choose a line spacing of 1.2 or bigger. And use a 'ragged' right-hand margin; this makes reading easier on the eye than having that margin 'justified' to the right.

■ If you have time, when you have a reasonably finished draft put it to one side and out of your conscious mind for two or three days, then print it out and read it. As you do so try to put yourself in the reader's shoes. Imagine that you are talking to your reader, and check that everything you are saying makes sense. You are very likely to find there are points you want to clarify.

Write good English

It is beyond the scope of this book (and its author) to teach you how to write well in English. There exist many style guides and manuals, both British and American, but these are best thought of as reference works. None of them is perfect or suits everybody (as you can see from reading reviews on the Amazon website). I suggest that you apply a practical test: when you have a language problem, look for advice on it in whatever books you can find in your library and bookshop, and choose the one that you find most helpful. I also suggest that you check out books on style by Joseph M. Williams, especially his *Style: Toward Clarity and Grace*.[7] The central objective of his book is 'to show how a writer quickly and efficiently transforms a rough first draft into a version crafted for the reader'. It does this brilliantly. Williams knows all about academic-speak and how to simplify it. It is a book to be read carefully from beginning to end rather than consulted when you have a problem.

Style

Here are some suggestions of my own about style.

- Don't write in a polemical, opinionated and/or emotion-laden style. Your writing should, as far as possible, be objective and dispassionate. An academic dissertation is not the place for you to display anger or contempt, or to apportion blame, or to be sarcastic or abusive. Nor is it the place for 'positive' emotions such as pleasure or congratulation.

- If your subject and approach call for you to make value judgments, save them for your Discussion. In that section, first take your reasoning as far as you can without being judgmental. Only then should you apply your personal judgments. And, when you do so, make it clear what criteria you are using, what the basis is for your judgments.

- Don't use expressions like 'I believe' and 'I think'. You do not get credit for your beliefs, and your thoughts need to be based on evidence, so cite that evidence and reason from it.

- Don't write in a chatty or journalistic style. ('Journalistic' tends to be used as a term of abuse among academics.) Try to use language in a rigorous and precise way. In the interest of user-friendliness, I have written this book using the informal language of spoken English as much as possible. You should not follow this example when writing your dissertation. It may lead you to be imprecise, and it may give an academic reader the impression that you are sloppy and non-rigorous in the way that you think.

- Don't try to write like a textbook or an authority on your subject. An academic may use expressions like 'We consider ...', 'In our judgment, ...', 'As So-and-so rightly says, ...', 'The evidence suggests ...'. (Evidence on its own suggests nothing whatever, of course. The accurate expression for an academic would be: 'In the light of this evidence and from my experience, I think ...'.) All these expressions carry the implication that he or she is an authority on the subject and not to be challenged. If you as a student use them, what you say and write may strike your teachers as pretentious and inappropriate.

- Don't use long, complicated sentences when you can use short ones. Your meaning will be clearer. And you know from your own experience of reading academic books and articles how infuriating it is when you have to translate complicated sentences into language that you can understand. It is not good practice to infuriate your readers.

- Don't use expressions like 'Many writers think ...'. The reader will immediately want to know who these 'many writers' are. So give their names and cite your sources.

- Your supervisor and his or her colleagues may have very definite views about style. If you are issued with a style guide, be sure to follow it. In particular, find out if it is acceptable for you to write in the first person. Can you say 'In this dissertation I shall show ...', 'I feel ...' and 'I conclude ...'? Or should you use impersonal forms, not using the word 'I' (or 'me'), such as 'This essay will show ...', 'The present writer feels ...' and 'One would conclude ...'?

- If you are familiar with American rather than the Queen's English and you would prefer to use American spelling in your dissertation, you must check with your supervisor that this departure from convention will be acceptable.

21

Dissertation: conforming to good academic practice

Referencing: citing your sources

Using other people's writings as sources and acknowledging their contribution by citing the source and saying where it is to be found – i.e. supplying a reference to it – is central to academic writing. It is good academic practice. It shows a proper concern on your part with the authority of the source and thus with its quality as 'material'. It also shows that you accept the obligation to make your reasoning transparent, open to scrutiny: in a sense this is your 'admission ticket' to the academic community. Citing your sources will enable the reader to check that you have used your sources appropriately and that your reasoning is sound, as well as doing justice to the original writer's moral claim to his or her 'intellectual property'. Citing your sources also protects you against possible accusations of plagiarism.

Using and citing sources involves providing three things:

■ Within your text, an extract from the source (a word-for-word quotation or your own paraphrasing of a quotation) or a statement of your own derived from the source.

■ Also within your text, an insert of some kind – a marker or 'cue' that directs the reader to a place where details of the source can be found.

■ Details of the source, i.e. where the original can be found.

Please note that there is no single correct style of referencing. Many dissertation handbooks instruct you to use one particular style. If you have a choice in the matter, your supervisor may express a preference. In some fields (medicine, law) there are standard styles in the UK and USA and other English-speaking countries, but in others there are not. Some publishers and journals have their own distinctive house style and there are some well-known texts available, too.[8,9]

Incorporate extracts into your text correctly

Short extracts

If you are quoting directly (rather than paraphrasing), and the extract is not more than a certain length – this could be two lines, three lines, 30 words or 40 words: check with your referencing style guide – enclose it in quotation marks. Check with your style guide, too, to see whether these should be single or double quotation marks. If the extract already includes a word, phrase or sentence in quotation marks, the guide may tell you that these should be double if the 'outside' ones are single, and vice versa.

Longer extracts

If your extract is longer than two or three lines, indent it. Your referencing style guide may tell you whether it should be indented from both margins or only the left-hand one. Do not enclose an indented extract in quotation marks.

Shortened extracts

It is permissible to shorten an extract by taking out words, so long as you do not change the author's meaning. (Never remove the word 'not', of course!) The fact that words have been taken out is shown by the insertion of (usually) three dots (i.e. full stops, or periods), also known as an ellipsis. You can enclose words of your own in place of the author's so that the extract still reads grammatically, but take care not to change the author's meaning; enclose your own words in square brackets [ ]. If, as a result of your shortening, a word that was formerly inside a sentence now begins one, enclose the first letter of that word, or the whole word, in square brackets. (Again, consult your referencing style guide – it may or may not require this.)

Paraphrasing

If you are paraphrasing someone else's work, it is important to make it clear that you are doing so; use some formula like 'to paraphrase X, ...'; 'X appears to be assuming/arguing/suggesting ...'; or 'in other words ...' (after an actual quotation).

The bewildering variety of referencing styles

There are, as far as I can see, four kinds of referencing style in general use. You can easily tell which is being used in a book or article that you're reading because they have different kinds of insert in the text. Look out for the following types.

- Author and date, e.g. Smith (1980) or (Smith, 1980). Full details of Smith's 1980 publication are contained in a list at the end of the book, the chapter or the article. I refer to this as the **author/date** style.

- Author and page number, e.g. Jones (117) or (Jones 117). I refer to this as the **author/page** style.

- Superscript, e.g. [12]. The superscript, or raised number, directs you to a footnote (at the foot of the page) or endnote (at the end of the book, chapter or article) with the same number. Full details of the publication are contained in the footnote or endnote. I refer to this as the **numbered-note** style. (The British Standards Institution describes it in BS 5605 : 1990 as the 'running notes' method.)[10] It is the style used in this book.

- Bracketed numbers, e.g. (12). Like the numbered-note style, the bracketed number directs you to a footnote (at the foot of the page) or endnote (at the end of the book, chapter or article) with the same number. The best-known version of this is the Vancouver style, but you'll also find it referred to as the 'numeric' style, so I refer to it as the **Vancouver-numeric** style. Unlike the numbered-note style, the same number (bracketed) may appear in more than one place in the text.

If you have some choice when it comes to selecting a referencing style, which one should you choose? Here are some things you should know about the four main kinds.

The author/date style

Varieties

In the UK and Australia the most common version of the author/date style is that known as the Harvard style. In the USA, the APA, ASA/

ASR and CBE and AIP styles are versions of this style.[11] It is commonly used in the physical and life sciences and the social sciences.

Inserts in the text

In the text you place an insert giving the author(s) and date of publication. For example: 'Smith (1980) describes X as ...' or 'X has been described (Smith, 1980) as ...'. If Smith had two publications in 1980, they are differentiated by putting letters (a, b ...) after the year. So if you are referring to both at different places, your text with inserts would look something like: 'Smith (1980a) describes ...' and 'Smith (1980b) concludes ...'. You might also want or be required to include page numbers, so that the reader does not have to wade through Smith's book in its entirety to find your source. Then your text with inserts would look something like: 'Smith (1980a, p.13) describes ...' or 'Some writers have concluded (e.g. Smith, 1980b: 17–18) ...'. Your style guide should tell you whether or not you are required to prefix page numbers by p. or pp., and whether it should be '(Smith, 1980)' or '(Smith 1980)'.

Listing

For every different insert, you write a reference saying where the source can be found. At the end of your essay you attach a list of all the references, in alphabetical order of authors' surnames. This list might be headed 'Bibliography', 'List of references' or 'Works cited'. There are a number of ways in which entries in the list could be set out – different style manuals prescribe different ones – but they all have in common that they begin something like: 'Smith, T. (1980) ...' and are in alphabetical order of authors' (or first author's) surnames. For a single-author book, the layout will usually be as follows:

Author's surname | Author's initials or first name | Year of publication | Title (usually in italics but may be underlined) | Number of edition if not the first | Place of publication (followed by a colon) | Publisher.

Usefulness

The author/date style is most useful where all your sources are books or journal articles with one or more designated authors. The insertion of dates in the text may be helpful, as Ritter points out, for following the progress of a debate.[12] This style also allows you to add or subtract references easily if you have occasion to amend your essay just before handing it in. It is less useful if you have to deal with 'messy' sources like newspaper articles and editorials, the publications of government bodies or other organizations where no author is credited, broadcasts on TV or radio, or websites. And it is of no use as a vehicle for 'parenthetical' comments – asides – that you don't want to place in the body of your essay.

The author/page style

Varieties

The main (if not the only) version of this style is the MLA style, codified by the Modern Language Association in the USA.

Inserts in the text

In the text you place an insert giving the author(s) and the number of the page or date of publication. For example: 'Jones (117) describes X as ...' or 'X has been described (Jones 117) as ...'. If you are referring to two different publications both authored by Jones, they are differentiated by including the title, which may be abbreviated.

Listing

At the end of your essay you attach a list of all the sources you have cited, in alphabetical order of authors' surnames. This list should be headed 'Works cited' and, like author-date lists, arranged in alphabetical order of authors' (or first author's) surnames. Thus, for a single-author book, the layout will usually be as follows:

Author's surname | Author's initials or first name | Year of publication | Title (usually in italics but may be underlined) | Number of edition if not the first | Place of publication (followed by a colon) | Publisher.

Usefulness

The author/page style is most useful where all your sources are books or journal articles with one or more designated authors. If your source is an article in a bulky newspaper, citing the page is good practice since it will help the reader to track down the article. It can also work satisfactorily even if no author is credited, because you can cite the title instead. It is less good with websites and, like the author-date style, is of no use as a vehicle for 'parenthetical' comments – asides – that you don't want to place in the body of your essay.

The Vancouver-numeric style

Varieties

The Vancouver style emerged from a meeting of editors of general medical journals in Vancouver, Canada, in 1978 to establish guidelines for the format of manuscripts submitted to their journals. The group agreed a set of guidelines that was first published in 1979 and defines the Vancouver style. The latest version, *Uniform Requirements for Manuscripts Submitted to Biomedical Journals*, is effectively the norm for biomedical journals. The numeric system described very briefly in *BS 5605 : 1990* is very similar.

Inserts in the text

At every point where you wish to supply a reference to a source that you have used, you insert a number in brackets (parentheses). (*BS 5605 : 1990* offers the choice of using superscripts instead.) Similarly to numbered notes, you start with (1), then (2), and so on, through the essay. *But* when you refer to a source that you have previously referred to, you insert its *original* number (*unlike* the numbered-note style). So if you refer to source no. 3 seven times, say, the insert (3) will appear seven times in your text.

Listing

For every insert, you write a reference saying where the source can be found. Your list of references will go at the end of your essay, in numerical order to correspond with the bracketed inserts. The list can appropriately be headed 'References'. For a single-author book, the layout of each one will be as follows:

> Author's surname | Author's initials or first name (but these can go before the surname if preferred) | Title (usually in italics but may be underlined) | Number of edition if not the first | Place of publication (followed by a colon) | Publisher | Year of publication.

Usefulness

Like the author/date style, the Vancouver-numeric style is most useful where all your sources are books or journal articles with one or more designated authors. The inserts are less distracting than authors, dates and page numbers. But if you have referred to different parts of the book in different places in your text it does not offer you an elegant method of citing the different page numbers in a book; it is therefore most effective where your sources are relatively compact, like journal articles or self-contained chapters in a book.

The Vancouver-numeric style is more economical than the numbered-note style in that only one reference is needed for each source (and so you will have no occasion to use *ibid.*, *op. cit.* or *loc. cit.*) But it is less useful if you have to deal with 'messy' sources, and it is of no use as a vehicle for parenthetical comments.

The numbered-note style

Varieties

Numbered-note styles include the Chicago and Turabian styles well known in the USA. In Australia, the so-called Oxford style and Cambridge style are also of this kind. In the UK, you may find it referred to as the traditional footnote style or the endnote style, or – as by the British Standards Institution – the 'running notes' style. It is commonly used in the arts and humanities, some social and political science fields, and law.

Inserts in the text

At every point where you wish to supply a reference or a comment of some kind, you insert a superscript, a raised number. You start with

[1], then [2], and so on, through the essay. Even if you are referring to a source that you have already referred to, you give it a new number. (So no superscript number appears twice.) Variants of this style place the footnote number in round or square brackets.

Listing

For every superscript, you write a note giving the reference and/ or making your comment. These notes may be placed at the foot of the page on which the superscript appears, in which case they are footnotes, or at the end of the essay, chapter or dissertation, in which case they are endnotes. The notes will be listed in numerical order to correspond with the superscripts. The list of endnotes can appropriately be headed 'Notes and references'.

In addition to the list of notes and references, you may be asked by your teachers to provide a Bibliography. Normally this would be a list of books and articles that you have used for 'background' reading; ask whether works listed in your notes should also be listed in your Bibliography.

If you are using the numbered-note style, your list will be arranged in the numerical order of your superscripts. This style does offer you some choice in laying out your references. For a single-author book, here are three possibilities:

Author's surname | Author's initials or first name | Title | Number of edition if not the first | Place of publication (followed by a colon) | Publisher | Year of publication | Page number(s).

Author's initials or first name | Author's surname | Title | Number of edition if not the first | Place of publication (followed by a colon) | Publisher | Year of publication | Page number(s).

Author's initials or first name | Author's surname | Year of publication (in brackets) | Title | Number of edition if not the first | Page number(s) | Place of publication (followed by a colon) | Publisher.

If you are using the numbered-note style, you may find yourself referring to the same source a number of times. There are conventions that you can use to save yourself copying out the reference afresh each time: the *'ibid.'*, *'op. cit.'* and *'loc. cit.'* conventions – *ibid*. is an abbreviation of *ibidem*, a Latin word meaning 'in the same place'; *op. cit*. is an abbreviation of *opere citato*, a Latin phrase meaning 'in the work cited'; *loc. cit*. is an abbreviation of *loco citato*, Latin for 'in the place cited'. (As you can see, I'm adopting the convention here of putting words that are in a foreign language in italics.) You can use *ibid*. when a note refers to the same source as does the previous note, either the same page or a different one. You can use *op. cit*. to refer to a work previously cited in the same list. And you can use *loc. cit*. when you are referring to the same place in a work previously cited in the same list. For example:

---

18 P. Levin (1997) *Making Social Policy*, p. 30. Buckingham: Open University Press.
19 *Ibid.*, p. 65. [Same author and book as in previous note but different page.]
20 *Ibid.* [Same author, same book and same page as in previous note.]
21 J.G. March and H.A. Simon (1958) *Organizations*, pp. 140–1. New York: Wiley.
22 Levin, *op. cit.*, p. 222. [The work by Levin previously cited in this list, but a different page.]
23 March and Simon, *loc. cit.* [The work by March and Simon previously cited in this list, and the same page.]

If the use of Latin strikes you as too archaic for words, you can do something like this:

---

18 P. Levin (1997) *Making Social Policy*, p. 30. Buckingham: Open University Press.
19 Levin, note 18, p. 65. [Same author and book as in previous note but different page.]
20 As note 19. [Same author, same book and same page as in previous note.]
21 J.G. March and H.A. Simon (1958) *Organizations*, pp. 140–1. New York: Wiley.
22 Levin, note 18, p. 222. [The work by Levin previously cited in this list, but a different page.]
23 As note 21. [The work by March and Simon previously cited in this list, and the same page.]

Usefulness

The great thing about the numbered-note style is that you can use it not only for references but for those parenthetical comments and asides that would interrupt the flow if you put them in the body of your text: a comment on the reliability of a source, or on some quirk that it exhibits; a reminder to the reader what certain abbreviations stand for; a signpost to another source where a different point of view can be found; and so on. It is also convenient to use when you are citing an original source that a 'secondary' source led you to: you can simply cite the original and then say 'cited by' the secondary source.

The numbered-note style can be cumbersome if you've inserted all your superscripts and then decide you want to add or subtract a reference, because this entails renumbering all the subsequent references. One way of getting round this is by using your word processor's automatic footnote/endnote system: another way is to type out each note within your text and enclose it within ## … ##: when you've finalized the text you can find these one by one, remove each one from the text on to the clipboard and substitute the relevant superscript, and then copy them from the clipboard in batches of ten into your 'Notes and references' list. While this technique is hardly at the forefront of technology, it is certainly an improvement on handwritten index cards. Don't forget to back up each time you add or modify a note.

Whichever referencing style you use, try to be 100 per cent accurate, complete and consistent in your referencing. In particular, pay attention to spelling authors' names correctly. A spellchecker won't help you with these, and errors in spelling names will give a poor impression to the reader.

Reference management software

There are now a number of versatile software packages – EndNote is probably the best known and most widely used – that will enable you to search online bibliographic databases, collect and manage references, and create in-text citations and bibliographies as you work, in whatever referencing format you choose. One of the benefits of using such a system should be that of consistency. Consult your institution's library to see what is available for you to use.

22

Avoiding plagiarism

Avoid accusations of plagiarism

'Plagiarism' is a hot topic in higher education. Cases have come to light of students presenting pieces of writing composed by other people as if these were their own work, i.e. without citing the actual source. Entire dissertations can be purchased on the internet, and there are cases of quantities of text being 'lifted' from an unacknowledged source and altered slightly in what can only have been an attempt to disguise the original source. Such actions are manifestly cheating – acting with the intention to deceive. The consequences can be very unpleasant. You may even be refused a degree or expelled from the institution and publicly branded as dishonest and a cheat. Definitely not recommended!

Higher education institutions have reacted to this situation by producing elaborate definitions of 'plagiarism' and detailed regulations on the subject; by investing in software that will detect similarities in wording between pieces of work on worldwide databases, and employing staff to look out for plagiarism (the 'plagiarism police'); and by issuing stern warnings couched in highly emotive language: plagiarism is a 'crime', 'stealing', the 'theft' of the original writer's property. (In fact, to 'steal' in English law is to take another person's property without permission and with the intention to deprive the owner of it; clearly plagiarism does not deprive the original writer of the use of his or her words. And even if you do acknowledge a writer whose words you use, you are not expected to contact him or her to ask their permission. Furthermore, should the original writer seek redress, their remedy lies in the civil law, not the criminal law. I find it strange that universities should be promulgating inaccurate facts and fallacious reasoning.)

Furthermore, the definitions and regulations are often highly confusing. There tends to be a common core – you mustn't pass off other people's work as your own, which is fair enough – but they all give rise to more questions. If you unintentionally don't cite a source, does that count as plagiarism? If you use a quotation and cite its source, but fail to put the quotation in quotation marks, or to indent it, are you plagiarizing? If you use two or three phrases that you dimly recollect from a lecture or seminar, or some article you've read, without attributing them, are you plagiarizing? How close to an unattributed original does paraphrasing have to be for it to be plagiarism? What counts as 'common knowledge', so you don't need to reference it? Academics give different answers to these questions. What will be plagiarism to one will be no more than poor academic practice to another. So what are you, as a student, to do?

The prime way of avoiding accusations of plagiarism is to conform to good academic practice. As I said in the opening paragraph to Chapter 21, that entails, when you're using other people's writings as sources, acknowledging their contribution by citing the source and saying where you found it, in sufficient detail for other people to find it, too. You will also protect yourself if you take the trouble to preface your dissertation with a paragraph in which you acknowledge ideas and suggestions that you have received from other sources, which could include lectures and seminars, as well as informal discussions.

Claim copyright for your work

If your dissertation is genuinely your own work, and you have properly acknowledged material drawn from other sources, copyright in it automatically belongs to you. You can state your claim to it by adding '© [Your Name] 2011' (or whatever the year is) at the foot of the title page. (In Microsoft Word, for © type [Ctrl] + [Alt] + [C].) You have done the work: you are entitled to take pride in being its author. And since it is not completely unknown for academics to get ideas from their students and pass them off as their own, a reminder about copyright won't be out of place.

Avoid collusion

You may find that you are warned not only against committing plagiarism but also against committing 'collusion', conspiring with one or more other students to improve your marks by working together. Of course, students have always worked together – these may be among your most memorable and valuable learning experiences – and today we have the bizarre situation in many UK universities that on the one hand they are actually encouraging students to develop their teamwork skills, yet on the other hand they are warning them against collusion!

How should you respond to these mixed messages? I would certainly encourage you to work with other students: you will learn from them as well as from your teachers, and you will usually be able to express ideas and ask questions without feeling that you are being judged, which may not be the case in 'official' tutorials, classes and seminars. But do stop short of drafting dissertations or parts of dissertations together. The final selection of words must emerge from your own mind – it must be your own.

And beware the temptation to be altruistic and show your work to somebody else who persuades you that they need help. If the other person copies some of your work, both you and they will be penalized if the copying is detected. And if the authorities are unable to say who is copying whom, you won't even gain credit for being the original author.

23

Dissertation: final editing

Final editing should involve no more than getting down to your word limit and giving the text a last check for clarity and style.

Get down to your word limit

Count up the words you've used (use your word processor's 'word count' tool). Re-read the regulations, and check that you know whether appendices, tables, footnotes, references, bibliography, etc. have to be included within the word limit. If the regulations are silent about these, you cannot be penalized for not including them.

If you find you're over the limit, do the following things:

- Look for repetition and cut it out as much as possible. Don't present data in a table and also give a verbal description of what is in the table: stick to giving your inferences from those data.

- See if there are any whole sections you can leave out. (There may be one or two that are interesting but won't earn you many marks: omit them.)

- Minimize description and direct quotations from the literature. These will earn you very few marks.

- Use short forms. Instead of 'It was found by Jones that ...', write 'Jones found that ...'

- Look carefully at phrases and sentences you have put in brackets (parentheses). You may be able to delete these without losing any meaning.

- See if you can remove any factual material from your text to a table or appendix, if it will thereby escape the word limit.

Check for clarity and style

In an ideal world, after completing your 'improved' draft, you will have a few days left before hand-in. Print out a copy, and leave it for a couple of days. (Take some exercise, catch up on your sleep, go to a movie.) Then read through your draft carefully, silently or out loud. Almost certainly you will find a few instances where you haven't made your meaning clear, or you haven't written in good English, or you've made a spelling mistake that your spellchecker hasn't picked up. Make the necessary corrections. Go back to Chapter 20, 'Improving your draft', find the suggestions under the subhead 'Style' (pages 112–13), and make any further changes that you feel would be advisable. Make sure the title page conforms to requirements and looks attractive. Now print out the final version and bind it.

That's it. Job done. Take pleasure in what you have achieved.

Notes and references

1. Faulkner may have been aware of the words of Graham Wallas – 'How can I tell what I think till I see what I say?' – in *The Art of Thought* (Jonathan Cape, 1926, p. 106), also used by E.M. Forster in *Aspects of the Novel* (Mariner Books, 1927), p. 101.
2. Peter Levin, *Write Great Essays!* (2nd edition, Open University Press, 2009).
3. As note 2. See Chapter 7 of that book: 'How to use the World Wide Web'.
4. The Copyright Licensing Agency Ltd (CLA), Notice: Photocopying, Scanning and Digital Re-use under the terms of the Higher Education Licence, 1 August 2008–31 July 2011. Online at: http://www.cla.co.uk/data/pdfs/he/ind_notice_for_display_comprehensive.pdf (accessed 9 October 2010).
5. Office of National Statistics, *What is Qualitative Research?* 'The term "qualitative research" is used to cover a wide range of approaches and methods. ... [The] general consensus is that qualitative research is a naturalistic, interpretative approach concerned with understanding the meanings which people attach to actions, decisions, beliefs, values and the like within their social world, and understanding the mental mapping process that respondents use to make sense of and interpret the world around them.' Online at: http://www.ons.gov.uk/about/who-we-are/our-services/data-collection-methodology/what-is-qualitative-research- (accessed 13 October 2010).
6. Table 6 is reproduced from *Write Great Essays!* (see note 2), pp. 102–3.
7. Joseph M. Williams, *Style: Toward Clarity and Grace* (University of Chicago Press, 1990).

8. C. Neville, *The Complete Guide to Referencing and Avoiding Plagiarism* (2nd edition, Open University Press, 2010).

9. R. Pears and G. Shields, *Cite Them Right* (8th edition, Palgrave Study Skills, 2010).

10. British Standards Institution (1990), *BS 5605 : 1990 Recommendations for citing and referencing published material* (London BSI, pp. 3–4). (This has been amended by BSI publication AMD 10182, published 15 December 1998.) See also British Standards Institution (2010), *BS ISO 690 : 2010 Information and documentation: Guidelines for bibliographic references and citations to information resources.*

11. APA = American Psychological Association; ASA/ASR = American Sociological Association/American Sociological Review; CBE = Council of Biology Editors; AIP = American Institute of Physics.

12. R.M. Ritter, *The Oxford Guide to Style* (Oxford University Press, 2002), p. 505.

Acknowledgments

To all of the many students who have discussed their dissertation with me, and the many who have attended my workshops at LSE. Without their questions, challenges, ideas and openness I could never have written this book.

To Liz Barnett, director of the Teaching and Learning Centre, LSE, for giving me the opportunity to continue working with students despite passing my official age of retirement and for tolerating occasional eccentricities, and to all my (now former) colleagues in the Centre for their affectionate support.

To George MacDonald Ross and Gillian Cleave, philosophers, for stimulating discussions, conducted in one case by email and in the other over the matrimonial dining table.

To anonymous academic reviewers to whose thoughtful suggestions for improving the first edition I hope I have done justice.